The Power
of Forgiveness

JEREMY P. TARCHER / PENGUIN

an imprint of Penguin Random House

New York

The Power of Forgiveness

Forgiving as a Path

to Freedom

JOAN GATTUSO

JEREMY P. TARCHER/PENGUIN
An imprint of Penguin Random House LLC
375 Hudson Street
New York, New York 10014

Copyright © 2015 by Joan Gattuso
Penguin supports copyright. Copyright fuels creativity, encourages
diverse voices, promotes free speech, and creates a vibrant culture. Thank you
for buying an authorized edition of this book and for complying with copyright
laws by not reproducing, scanning, or distributing any part of it in any form
without permission. You are supporting writers and allowing Penguin to
continue to publish books for every reader.

Most Tarcher/Penguin books are available at special quantity discounts
for bulk purchase for sales promotions, premiums, fund-raising, and educational
needs. Special books or book excerpts also can be created to fit specific needs.
For details, write: SpecialMarkets@penguinrandomhouse.com.

ISBN 978-0-399-16314-2

Printed in the United States of America
1   3   5   7   9   10   8   6   4   2

Book design by Gretchen Achilles

Some names and identifying characteristics have been changed
to protect the privacy of the individuals involved.

Contents

I lovingly dedicate this book to all
my teachers of forgiveness.

Introduction

I first spotted him when my husband, David, and I were staying temporarily in a tiny condo at the Pacific Ocean, waiting to find our perfect permanent home. We had finally realized our long-held dream to move to Molokai, one of the more rural of the Hawaiian Islands.

Returning after dark to the condo, we passed the laundry room, which was glaring with light. In the center of this bright space sat a man in a wheelchair, his physical body covered by burn scars and grafted skin. An attendant was hovering near him. Before I was able to feel compassion for him, I found myself feeling aghast at his appearance and immediately forced myself to look away. Who I saw there I couldn't quite comprehend.

My rational mind then decided he must be the survivor of an explosion in a war zone—perhaps Iraq, perhaps Afghanistan. The fleeting image of him stayed with me through the night.

The next day I was enjoying myself at the pool, chatting with a friend's mother, a woman I had known from previous visits to the island. I brought up the man in the laundry room, and she told me his name was W Mitchell (no period after the W) and he had written a very uplifting book about not one but two horrific experiences that had left him in his present physical state. He hadn't been in a war, but he had gone through hell.

The woman lent us Mitchell's book, *It's Not What Happens to You, It's What You Do About It*. I quickly devoured it, as did David. We were both moved deeply by the inner strength of this man. As you will discover later in these pages, Mitchell has what one could only call an enlightened view of forgiveness.

His story is one of many that have inspired this book. I believe that telling stories of forgiving and forgiveness— my own stories as well as others'—helps all of us to experience the power of forgiveness in our own lives. For example . . .

Few of us in our lives will encounter anything like the Chinese communist regime that murdered one million Tibetans, destroyed six thousand of their temples, and took over their country. But one man, one of the holiest on our planet, faced just such horror.

At a young age His Holiness the Dalai Lama had to face the overthrow of his nation of Tibet—high in the Himalayas, a deeply spiritual, peaceful, and feudal land. The Chinese army of Mao invaded and, with total lack of respect for everything these gentle, nonviolent people stood for, began the systematic dismantling of their monastic hierarchic culture, their language, their customs, and their homeland.

Now, more than six decades after the invasion, the Dalai Lama is at peace with the suppression of his people. He doesn't in any way agree with it, but when he recounts the years of anguish and suffering, he becomes philosophical. Soon after the overthrow he came to realize that any hatred of the Chinese communists would only pollute his own soul. This realization was a process for him, just as it is a process for us all.

I have been extremely blessed to have been in his presence and at his teachings a number of times since 1991. Each encounter has been deeply meaningful and life enriching for me. On these occasions I know I am in the presence of a holy man who demonstrates, every second of his life, what we are all meant to be. He shows us the way to what we all can become—of what we all must become—if we are to establish peace once and for all on our planet.

This holy man holds no animosity in his heart in spite of the terrible acts visited on his people. Why? Because he thoroughly practices the power of forgiveness. He is able to advance along the spiritual path by leaps and bounds while forgiving the atrocities inflicted on his fellow monks and citizens. Perhaps his example can help you to forgive your brother or sister.

When we examine what he has accomplished in forgiveness, given the incredible severity of his situation, can you see how trivial your unforgiven situation can seem within the great scheme of life itself?

Some folks wear T-shirts and bracelets with the initials *WWJD* (What Would Jesus Do?). Now think about a situation in your life that requires the healing power of forgiveness toward someone you feel has harmed you. Ask yourself:

- What would His Holiness the Dalai Lama do?
- What would a spiritual teacher do?
- What would a holy person do?
- What would a spiritually awake person do?
- What would the most aware person you know do?
- What would and should you do?

Remember, you don't do forgiveness work to change the other person. Most likely that will never happen. You engage in these practices to change *you*.

In order to forgive, we have to be willing to move beyond our pain, to give up our story, to stop being the victim, to become the victor. The Dalai Lama has said that he learned that through forgiveness his mind could become clear and calm.

Forgiveness works more effectively to bring forth desired outcomes than do anger and hatred. I love this simple formula the Dalai Lama teaches to attain happiness:

First, we learn through meditation to empty the mind.

Second, in this empty mind (called "clear light") compassion is now generated.

Third, compassion meets emptiness, and the result is happiness.

As a formula: emptiness + compassion = happiness

For many of us emptiness is a difficult concept to comprehend. For those whose spiritual path incorporates the spiritual and psychological teachings found in the sacred text called *A Course in Miracles*, I believe it is considerably easier to understand emptiness. In reading that text, one comes to understand that what we call "seeing" is not really *seeing* what is truly in front of us, because our minds are nearly always focused on thoughts from the past. *A Course in Miracles* instructs us to learn that we really do not know what anything is for, that we have invented it all, seeing the world through our fear rather than through what's really there, a situation it calls "madness." And it teaches that beyond all this fear-based madness is peace, and also that beyond all this madness is emptiness. In Judeo-Christian terms we can say that beyond all this self-made madness, we will find God. The formula now looks like this:

$$God + compassion = happiness$$

Another way of understanding this concept of emptiness is to say that everything you deal with—your home, your work, your car, your bank account, your education, etc., etc., etc.—has no meaning. Rather, we have assigned meaning to all of it, but that does not make any of it true or real.

When we grasp the concept that all things are empty of meaning, and we marry that idea with compassion, then—voilà!—we experience happiness.

For example, let me tell you about a woman I consider a close friend, even a soul sister. This woman has a brother who is stuck in negativity and is often mean to his family, and especially to her. He makes up outlandish tales about her, and their family, and then broadcasts them to all who will listen. For years she endured his cruelty.

It was through the practice of forgiveness that she has come to a place in her life where his attacks no longer penetrate her psyche. She knows absolutely that there is no substance to his words of accusation. His words and actions are empty. Forgiveness has bathed her in compassion; thus, she can be happy and continue to be happy regardless of his or anyone's antics.

In *The Wisdom of Forgiveness*, the Dalai Lama writes, "Compassion is the best source of happiness for a happy world and a happy life. There is no doubt."

In a conversation with the Dalai Lama, Victor Chan, founder of the Dalai Lama Center for Peace and Education, said to him, "Forgiveness is in your bones."

Throughout *The Power of Forgiveness* we will explore at its very depths what true forgiveness is and how each of us can arrive at an enlightened state of mind. Forgiveness can be in our bones as well.

Many of us have been deeply wounded by others' unskilled behaviors—be it one individual or many, through racism, ethnic cleansing, physical violence, or cruel psychological attacks—all threatening to erode our spiritual essence. We've been hurt by family or friends, by groups or politics or violence. We've been hurt by criticism, unfair judgments, unkind people. Perhaps we've also hurt others.

The Power of Forgiveness will give you potent and effective spiritual tools to help you dismantle your hurt, grievances, and suffering so you can heal the past and live a fully enlightened life.

CHAPTER 1

Forgiveness Offers Everything I Want

It is through forgiveness that true spiritual
healing is accomplished.

—CHARLES FILLMORE, *cofounder of Unity*

On June 11, 1963, a Vietnamese Buddhist monk did the unthinkable—but for a very spiritual reason. His name was Thich Quang Duc and he was sixty-six years old. He had entered the monastery at age fifteen and was ordained as a monk at twenty.

Thich Quang Duc was deeply disturbed by the war in his country. There appeared to be no way to stop the horror. His people were being slaughtered, not only young men bearing arms, but old men, young women, and children.

The leadership on all sides appeared to be asleep to the horrors in their very midst. What could a simple monk do? He had to get the authorities' attention in a manner nothing else could.

He sought a course of action.

For several weeks, he meditated constantly, clearing his mind so that an appropriate answer would emerge.

The idea came, and he put it into form. First he wrote to government leaders on all sides. He also wrote letters to Christian churches and Buddhist monasteries about why he had reached what most considered a shocking decision. One letter he wrote said: "Before closing my eyes and moving toward the vision of the Buddha, I respectfully plead to President Ngo Dinh Diem to take a mind of compassion toward the people of the nation and implement religious equality to maintain the strength of the homeland eternally. I call the venerables, reverends, members of the sangha and the lay Buddhists to organize in solidarity to make sacrifices to protect Buddhism." Zen Buddhist teacher Thich Nhat Hanh said that Thich Quang Duc's letters were almost love letters because his desire to communicate was so intense.

For Thich Quang Duc "closing my eyes" meant death by self-immolation. His determination to get the attention of the authorities and the world was guaranteed. Nothing else would have ever come close.

He consciously chose an extreme teaching example motivated by love. Many people, especially in the Western world, thought he was crazy. However, while I'm in no way advocating we take the same dramatic actions he took, I don't believe he was crazy. He was holy. He simply knew that his extreme action as an attempt to bring peace was infinitely more important than his physical existence. Perhaps he was on his path to enlightenment.

His story, motivation, and actions are not so dissimilar from those of Mahatma Gandhi, who would go to peaceful extremes to get the attention of the British Empire, which ruled India at the time; or Jesus Christ, who was willing to walk to Calvary to his own execution; or many others down through human history. They saw their lives embracing a larger story than their individual personalities. Their acts were not of the ego; rather, each had an enormous heart that was willing to do whatever it took to transform the hatred in all its manifestations prevalent in the era in which they lived.

Thich Quang Duc and others' shocking examples are sentinels that point the way to wake up and live life differently so that their supreme acts will not be in vain. Through them, we can perhaps see that the ones we consider as enemy we can now begin to see as friend, even brother or sister. This is forgiveness in action.

I look at Thich Quang Duc's selfless act as the beginning of the end of the Vietnam War. We are not to self-immolate like him, but we can look deeply within and ask ourselves, What would you have me do, what would you have me say, in order to live my life differently? What would you have me do to end this blinding sense of separation so I can be healed?

Waking up to our own path, and to the process of forgiveness, can often come through the experiences we have. What have your experiences been that caused you to begin waking up? It takes a tremendous amount of energy to get us to wake up out of our spiritual slumber individually and collectively. And if we wish to wake up more fully, then it's vital we keep on with our prayer work, our spiritual study, our meditations, our forgiveness work.

> *The human heart can go to the lengths of God.*
> *Dark and cold we may be, but this*
> *Is no winter now. The frozen misery*
> *Of centuries cracks, begins to move,*
> *The thunder is the thunder of the floes,*
> *The thaw, the flood, the upstart Spring.*
> *Thank God our time is now when wrong*
> *Comes up to face us everywhere,*
> *Never to leave us till we take*
> *The longest stride of soul men ever took.*
> *Affairs are now soul size.*
> *The enterprize*
> *Is exploration into God.*
> *Where are you making for?*
> *It takes*

So many thousand years to wake,
But will you wake for pity's sake?

—CHRISTOPHER FRY, *A Sleep of Prisoners*

There are ways to break through into greater aware-ness. There are ways to become what God intended us to be.

My dear friend Ric, a tall, lean man, was involved in a horrific auto accident. Multiple bones were broken on impact. The healing process of his body was not a quick one. Several orthopedic surgeries followed, one after the other. In between the operations he recuperated in a reha-bilitation facility. There he was faced with a great deal of free time—free time that he decided to put to positive spiritual use.

Ric began meditating several hours a day. One day, while in a deep state, he began to witness an internal light, a sapphire beam that began to radiate through his injured right side. He observed it as its intensity grew, and he allowed himself to be bathed in that light. After several minutes he was filled with the awareness that his bones would mend, his body would heal, and his life would one day return close to what it had been.

When Ric came out of the meditation, he was filled with awe, wonder, and gratitude. His gratitude came from his having been a lifelong faithful practitioner and minister of spiritual principles, including deep forgiveness. He knew that when he had a physical or spiritual healing crisis and the need for a miracle, there it was, complete with the reassurance: All is well.

A Dramatic Story of the Power of Forgiveness

Of the many, many stories regarding forgiveness that I have personally encountered over the years, the following one is the most horrific.

Marcia was a member of the spiritual center I founded and where I was spiritual director for nearly thirty years. A beautiful, statuesque woman who always dressed like she was the mother of the bride, she was employed as a social worker, caring for the homeless at a local shelter. At the time she was exercising a couple of times a week with a personal trainer, Mike, also a social worker.

They eventually began to date, their relationship became more serious, and in time he moved in with her into her home. From the moment he moved in, all was not bliss. She quickly discovered that he was very controlling, beyond what she could imagine. She was not looking for someone to control her.

The lopsided relationship continued for several months until, on New Year's Day, she told him she was done and he had to move out. Surprisingly, he resisted very little at first. Then Marcia moved him out—she found an apartment for him, paid the first month's rent, and paid for his move. She said to him that their contact was over and added, "There is no going back and forth."

After she returned to her life, which included graduate school, Mike appeared at her door and asked to borrow her car so he could attend an out-of-town conference. She told him no. Then he asked if he could borrow it locally to let others know he couldn't drive to the meeting. Since his work involved reuniting incarcerated fathers with their children, a cause she found inspiring, Marcia reluctantly agreed. He left, and he returned with the car less than a half hour later. When he handed her the keys he leaned in to her and tried to kiss her. She pushed him away and said, raising her voice, "Didn't I tell you we were done? It doesn't work like this anymore." And he said, "I'm sorry," and he left.

Marcia continues the story: "About half an hour later a male friend, who was a locksmith, came to change the locks in my house, since Mike would never give me back the keys after we broke up, which had been over a year. So my friend started changing the locks, and I got dressed for work. Then my best friend, Sheryl, called, and I talked with her for about fifteen minutes. I was sitting at the kitchen table, and I saw Mike coming up the driveway. I said to Sheryl, 'You're not going to believe this, but

Mike is walking up the driveway.' She said, 'What does he want?' I said, 'I don't know, but I'm not going to let him in the house. I don't want his energy in here anymore.' She said, 'Good.' Then I asked her to stay on the phone while I went to the door. Sheryl said, 'Be strong. Don't let him in the house.' I told her I wouldn't. So I went to the door, opened it, and he shot me in the face.

"Sheryl couldn't tell I'd been shot, but she knew something had happened. After I fell Mike kicked me, and my locksmith friend . . . heard me moan. The locksmith then came to the door with my dog, Brownie. He saw that Mike was about to shoot me again in the back of the head. Mike spotted him and began to chase him as my friend then ran into my bedroom, broke out a window, and jumped out and ran to a convenience store around the corner. He told the clerk behind the counter to lock the door and call the police. Sheryl called a female friend who lived a few doors down, and that friend and the ambulance arrived at the same time. When my neighbor friend saw me, she thought I was dead because I was blue.

"I've always been in disbelief that I was shot, since I don't have any direct memory of the experience. The details of it are all from other people. What makes me know it's real are the physical ailments I have as a result of it."

Marcia wasn't expected to live. She later was told that seven out of ten people who experience such a traumatic injury die on the way to the hospital. Almost all the rest die within forty-eight hours. Few thought Marcia would survive. Marcia says, describing the destructive path of the small missile: "The bullet entered my left cheek, shattered the mandible, severed the fifth cranial nerve, severed the left optic nerve, severed an artery, and lodged itself in C1, the first vertebra. That's where the bullet remains.

"I have no memory of being taken to the hospital," she says—or of the first three weeks she spent there. "But I knew I was in a Chinese restaurant. I like Chinese food. Maybe that's why my mind went there. I felt like I had been in this restaurant before. It may have been China Gate, which has been torn down. I was lying on a table in the restaurant, and I wondered, 'Why in the world am I lying on this table?'

"Tenetta, a friend of mine who's into Chinese herbs and the like, was working on me while I was on the table. She wasn't speaking to me, just healing me. She was rubbing herbs on my right arm, the arm that was paralyzed. In my dream state I didn't know my arm was paralyzed. I was just fine. Sheryl was on my other side by my shoulder, and every time I would try to get up Sheryl would lightly touch my shoulder and say, 'No, not yet.' I would ask, 'When, when?' And she would respond gently, 'Not yet, not yet.' Later on I sat up, but I never got off the table. All my family and friends and people from church were there too, but they were behind a Japanese silk screen. I could hear them and see them, but I couldn't make them out as individuals. I think that was really happening in my hospital room. Sheryl said that so many people came to see me, the hospital staff had to limit the number in the room. I figured that must have been the screen I saw—the limiting of the number of people."

The physicians tending her felt she had little chance of recovery. If she lived she would probably be a vegetable. She was on life support. She breathed through a tracheostomy tube, and it was assumed she was brain-dead. To make matters even worse, her bullet injury caused a stroke, leaving her paralyzed on her right side.

The miracle that happened was that one day, after three weeks, several doctors were in her room discussing removing Marcia from life support. Her friend Sheryl was in the room and saw a tear making its way down Marcia's cheek. Getting rid of life support was then no longer an option, and shortly after that Marcia awoke.

Once she awakened, her recovery had just begun. She had to learn to walk again. She had to learn to speak again. She had trouble remembering. She had very little stamina.

But she was determined to walk again, to talk again, to live as close to a normal life as possible. Months and months of rehabilitation followed. But eventually she walked, she talked, and she went back to work and back to school for an advanced degree.

Clearly, what Mike did was horrendous, and he was

sentenced to prison for a number of years. Her friends and family told her it was an unforgivable act—but Marcia wanted to be free from the effect this experience had on her. Marcia knew she had much forgiveness work to do—on herself as well as Mike. She began using the forgiveness practices that we will discuss in this book and decided she no longer wanted to live a life of blame and anger. She had to let it go. Marcia is the first to tell you that she found much of the forgiving work difficult, and she faltered in some of her future relationships. But she stayed the course, kept forgiving, and continued pursuing her spiritual life.

The power of forgiveness worked for Marcia. She eventually became a prayer practitioner in her Unity church. She started a new life in California. She is now in a holy relationship with a loving, caring man she met at church. She is now her own person, happy and free and ready to forgive anything that comes up against her. She no longer has the need to rescue dysfunctional men, and she refuses to ever be the victim again. Forgiving set her free to fly higher than ever before.

How I Used the Power of Forgiveness

Yes, you can forgive and love, and it is more positive than planning how to get even with someone or figuring out ways to look clever or act superior to the person you find it hard to forgive. You can choose peace over pain. As the Dalai Lama has said (I suspect with tongue slightly in cheek), "Look at one person who annoys you, and use the opportunity to counter your own anger and cultivate compassion. But if the annoyance is too powerful—if you find the person so repulsive that you cannot bear to be in his or her presence—it may be better to look for the exit!"

There is a most interesting fact about having a painful thought. I've read that a painful thought actually vibrates in our bodies and minds with energy of its own accord for about ninety seconds. Then it's up to us. We can choose to let it go, and go on with our lives, or we can choose to keep it alive by re-creating it again and again by giving it our undivided attention.

Believe me, we have all done this, and probably numerous times. One of my latest examples came from the death of an active congregant from my church. She was a true character, a nurse at the city jail who loved being where she was. This was a job most people wouldn't want at twice the pay, but she did. She took no guff from anyone, she had an opinion about everything, and the inmates loved her. Members of her spiritual community loved her as well.

After her sudden passing, I went with my husband and a practitioner from church to visit with the woman's two daughters to offer our love and condolences. Two days later the daughters and I met to formulate their mother's memorial service.

I do a highly personal service that weaves together details of the life of the deceased with reflections from loved ones. Appropriate music and meditation round out the service.

I spent many hours gathering all the information and creating a beautiful service for this very loved member. Over 250 mourners were in attendance at the funeral home. The service was meaningful and beautiful. Afterward the mourners came to the lower level of our church for a reception in a space that is not ours but belongs to a different church we rent from and share space with. Because we don't own the space, the family paid the $325 fee to rent the space from the other church.

It all went exactly as planned—except that I wasn't paid for my ministerial services. After a couple of weeks my assistant called and left a message about the nonpayment but never received a return call. About a week after that I called and left a message. Soon after, the older sister returned the call, and after exchanging pleasantries she informed me that they had already paid $325, thinking that amount covered the entire funeral, not just renting the space. I attempted to explain that it was a separate fee, paid to the other church for the space only, and didn't cover my time and expenses to create and perform the funeral service. When I was done explaining this, there was silence on the phone. After waiting a few moments for her response, it dawned on me that she had hung up.

I was flabbergasted, and just then my assistant came into my office. In shock I said, "She hung up on me! That's never happened to me in my entire life." I think I repeated "She hung up on me!" about a half dozen times. I was trying to wrap my brain around the fact that a member of a family I had done so much for had hung up on me. I was exhibiting what the Buddhists would call "unskilled behavior."

When I returned to my usually centered self, the realization came that I was upset not so much about not getting paid for all my caring, time, and effort as I was that someone would think it was appropriate to hang up on anyone.

My church board wanted me to invoice the sisters. I declined to do so because, as I told the board, they already knew it was their moral and spiritual obligation to pay me, or any minister, for services rendered.

What was I to do with this woman who irritated me? I wanted to move on but found that I wasn't letting the irritation go. That was when I realized that I had to set a course to do more forgiveness work. Here's what I did.

First, I began meditating on this current upset. Within a short amount of time, it became clear that it would be healing to write a letter to this woman who'd hung up on me, to express my feelings at being so disrespected by someone I had embraced and to whom I'd given so very much of my time. Of course, this was one of those letters that I would never mail. Why? Because writing the letter was for me, to give me a sense of clearing out my hurt and anger, and to empty myself of the story that I had created around it.

Why does writing a letter help? For years I have found writing—in a variety of forms—to be most helpful at moving blocked emotions and energy. After finishing the letter I decided, in order to more fully let the upset go, it would be best to burn it and watch it go up in flames and dissolve into ash. I set up a safe place to light the paper on fire, and watching it burn, I breathed deeply through the whole process. When only ashes remained, I found that my anger had dissipated and peace had returned to my mind and body. Those daughters never paid me, but God certainly has.

Do you have someone who you find hard to forgive? Try writing a letter—either write it on paper to be safely burned, dissolved, or destroyed, or write it in the safety of your private journal. (Turn to the end of this chapter for more instruction. A "Forgiveness in Action" exercise is included at the end of each chapter.)

Forgive Them, for They Know
Not What They Do

Spiritually we are well-advised to have a soul teacher or mentor to look to as an example of what we are to do when we find ourselves in these tight, uncomfortable spots in life. If you choose Jesus, follow him—not to the cross but to the resurrection. In *A Course in Miracles* it says: "Each day, each hour and minute, even each second, you are deciding between the crucifixion and the resurrection; between the ego and the Holy Spirit."

In this situation, where I felt someone had disrespected me, my ego was bruised and slapped around, and it was pretty much living in outrage. I had to tame that beast in order to return to peace and experience tranquility once again.

We can say with Jesus, "Father, forgive them, for they know not what they do." We can learn to absorb these words on two levels. The first is to interpret Jesus's words at face value. The person who has hurt another is often ignorant of that fact, unaware that his or her words or actions have wounded another. This individual is living in an unconscious state, not aware of the arrows he or she is shooting out. The second way to interpret Jesus's words is to understand that the one who shoots the arrows is, above all else, actually wounding himself deeply. Although unaware of what is happening in spiritual reality, this person is crying out for love and help, not punishment, condemnation, and further separation. It takes tremendous compassion and practice to forgive on this deeper level.

Your unloving thoughts about any person or situation are keeping you in a hell of your own making. It is forgiveness that lifts you out of your self-made hell and guides you into the light. Through forgiveness you demonstrate your release from your self-imposed prison. Through forgiveness you can think clearly, and the memory of who and what you are returns to your mind. Forgiveness acknowledges your holiness, your magnitude, your oneness with God. If it is liberation you want, forgiveness liberates your soul.

You will now find peace.

When we forgive, we remember who we are. When we hold on to grievances, we forget. Just feel the simple power in these statements of truth.

I think of the legions I have known who have made such misery for themselves because they cannot get over a hurt from the past. Their constant reliving of an event has kept it ever alive in their mind and psyche, and in this way they continue to keep themselves in hell.

If people could only understand the power they possess and the power of their thoughts, they could change their lives for the better. The great philosopher Ralph

Waldo Emerson said that we become what we think about all day long. As we continue to hold on to our grievances, we continue to keep ourselves in misery and hell. We are then living in an illusion about ourselves and not living in the truth of our being.

That truth is this. You are a spiritual being, living in a spiritual world, governed by spiritual law. Remember, you always have a choice. You have free will, and your choice is to either turn toward the light—the spirit—or turn toward the constant confusion of the ego.

Your ego will always instruct you that it is right to hold on to grievances, that forgiveness is folly. It is your ego that instructs you that what another person or another group or another culture has done is unforgivable. Adhering to this belief not only keeps the ego alive but prevents you from experiencing the shift in perception and the peace of mind that forgiveness will bring.

From *A Course in Miracles*: "If you but knew the glorious goal that lies beyond forgiveness, you would not keep hold on any thought, however light the touch of evil on it may appear to be." Forgiveness removes you from the evil dream of what has been done to you, and this act alone releases you, offering you freedom, liberation, healing.

When we hold fast to a grievance about another, we will always see ourselves and the other as separate. Separation is a perception, not a reality. Perception keeps us engaged in a constant process of evaluation—good/bad, more/less, desirable/undesirable—an ongoing round of accepting and rejecting. Everything is always changing. Perceptions are based on false evidence.

Think of perceptions as a cosmic game of smoke and mirrors. All may look a certain way, but is it really? Perceptions at best give us the tiniest glimpse of what may be going on. Beyond perceptions lies knowledge, but we can achieve knowledge only when we have released all our perceptions. This is no easy task.

Knowledge is permanent. It never changes. It has no degrees as perception does. Our perceptions disappear in the light as knowledge dawns in our minds, and they then return to their original unsullied state of holiness.

At times our perceptions can be accurate, but more often than not they offer us a very mixed bag—perhaps a mixed bag with a sprinkling of the eternal, but most often simply a confused mixed bag of misperceptions.

When you enter into the state of mind where knowledge abides, you experience liberation. You are no longer bound to false "facts" or false images your perceptions have given you. Knowledge can dawn in your consciousness only when you have become aware of the illusions that have been governing you.

Our minds cannot be host to illusions and the truth simultaneously. When we live mostly asleep, spiritually, we confuse the two and cannot clearly distinguish one from the other. Truth can dawn only on an unclouded mind. We can only know oneness or dwell ignorantly in illusions. When we recognize our oneness with God, we then know we dwell in the mind of God.

When a spiritual practitioner of mine was once leading a class for me, one of the students piped up and with great authority said, "I don't believe God has a mind." The teacher responded, "No, God does not have a mind like you and I have a mind. Rather, God is Mind. God is the totality of the universe. God is not a man or a woman, nor does God have a mind like a man or a woman. God is the vastness of the cosmos and so much more. But in our grasping to understand this esoteric concept we must use words we understand and then expand upon them."

A Course in Miracles contains a single idea that has lit up my life: "God has given you a place in His Mind that is yours forever." When we embrace this awesome truth, how can we ever be bereft or lonely or lost? You and I dwell in the mind of God. How can we nurse a hurt or hold on to a grievance when we glimpse the truth of our being?

My metaphysical friends and colleagues with some frequency ask this rhetorical question: How can people sustain themselves in the face of adversity and hardship if they do not have an unshakable faith in and an awareness of their oneness with God?

Andrew is the second husband of my dear friend Carole. Carole and I were classmates and roommates when we traveled together on a teenage tour of Europe. And although we may go for a year without talking, we have remained good friends. She is a friend like Confucius described when he wrote, "Good friends are like stars . . . you don't always see them, but you know they are there." Carole is always there for me, and I for her.

Carole's first husband, Gregg, died young after battling cancer for several years. They had no children. Although Carole was devastated by her loss, she found solace in her faith and her church community. There she met Andy, who was living through an unspeakable horror.

Andy had been happily married and the father of two young girls. He was an attorney who represented their church's district headquarters. This family of four lived a bonded, loving, happy life in their small New England community.

One day the incomprehensible happened. Andy, though he tried to call several times, could not reach his wife by phone. When he returned home he was greeted by an eerie quiet. Calling out to his wife and daughters he got no response. He ran upstairs to the master bedroom and found his beloved wife dead in a pool of blood on their marital bed. He fell to his knees, frozen in disbelief. He slowly arose and held her, as he screamed and sobbed.

Then the thought of his daughters shocked him into action. He jumped up and raced to their bedroom. It was empty. Then he went to the bathroom, where he found both of his precious daughters drowned in the bathtub. When he called the police, at first he couldn't speak. The horror was more than the human mind could grasp.

As time passed, Andy went through the motions of living. He spent a great deal of time attempting to begin the healing process after the violent murder of his family. It came to light that an extremely deranged teenager had been obsessed with his wife and daughters. Unknown to Andy and his family, this sick young man had crept into their home and was living during the day between the walls. He was skinny and was able to slip between the exterior and interior walls and spy on the family. No one had a clue that this creepy scenario was going on almost daily.

After the tragedy, weeks turned into months, and months into years. Eventually Andy joined a grief support group in his church, where he met Carole. He had barely known her before, but both of them leaned on the others in the support group—and eventually on each other.

Andy was traumatized to his core, but he was a man of deep faith, and in time the horror and images began to fade just a bit, and he could open himself up to love again. As Carole's grief also began to wane, their friendship began to grow. First it was a casual coffee date, then lunch, then a homemade dinner from Carole, then long walks and movies and dinner out.

Inch by inch a degree of normalcy eased into their lives. They had much in common, not just their shared grief but also their values and belief and faith. And the love deep within these two remarkable people began to bloom for each other.

A number of years ago, when Carole and I met for the day when I was vacationing in New England, I asked her if she thought Andy would agree to my interviewing him for a column I was writing. She looked down, shook her head no, and said, "Not yet. He's just not ready." Some years later I asked her the same question again. Her answer was the same. "Not yet. He's not ready."

Is someone who has been through a trauma that nearly ripped his soul out of his body ever ready to truly begin the journey of forgiveness? But without forgiveness the terror continues to stay alive. I am not delusional. Neither you nor I can comprehend what Andy's soul has had to endure, what images haunt his mind. And yet I know that there is someplace beyond this atrocity, a realm of undisturbed peace deep within Andy. I don't know if Andy has ever touched that place or not, but I know it's a very real place.

Spiritually we are reminded that our minds are one with God's. That part of our mind can never be defiled. Through the traumas, trials, and tribulations of life we can, with a high degree of openness and much practice, discover that part of our mind, the part that has never been defiled or left its home in God. How freeing, how liberating, how glorious. The truth is in you. The truth is in Andy. The truth is in the troubled teenager whose insanity turned to murder. In realizing that truth, we can find a way to forgive; and in forgiving, we can touch that place of truth.

The Light Has Come

When you find yourself deeply troubled by a situation, it is good to sit quietly, closing your eyes and affirming softly over and over again:

The light has come. I will there be light.

Affirm this truth over and over and darkness and despair will disappear. If the light has come, disaster must disappear. You can now be at peace, for the light has come.

You see a world undefiled, different and at peace because the light has come. Forgive and this is the pristine world you will see as you forgive the world. Dwell not on your past pain now. Be willing to forgive it all and be washed clean of every grievance and false belief. Forgive the world. Forgive yourself for every mistaken conception, for every dark belief that your ego held out to you.

Consider the New Testament story of Jesus going into

the wilderness to pray. There he is tempted. The unen-lightened think it is the devil tempting Jesus. A more en-lightened view is that it is Jesus's own ego, tempting him to separate himself from God and choose worldly power over heaven.

Doing one short prayer affirmation—*The light has come*—has brought me and countless others a clear per-ception of the world, a remembrance of what we once knew in our innocence. By repeating over and over this affirmation you will begin to see differently. As you rec-ognize that the light has come, the world and you are re-leased from the darkened dreams of the ego mind. You will no longer be tempted by the ego to join it in a hellish state of mind. This is one of the enormous gifts forgive-ness offers you.

What happened to Andy? Sadly, he died in 2014. An extremely fast-growing cancer presented itself five months before his death, and in spite of his heroic attempt to bat-tle it, the cancer raged through his body. He eventually came home from the hospital for the last time, and al-though he was told he would have six to eight weeks at best, he lived only ten more days. Ten days is time enough to say good-bye and short enough that the suffering does not become unbearable for all. Andy went peacefully into the night. He went peacefully home to God. For Andy we could say, "The light has come."

Carole now has her spiritual tools to call upon once

again for strength. Right view. Right thought. Right action. These Buddhist tenets can bring you strength. Carole has a solid faith in God and is surrounded by a supportive spiritual community. These are very helpful. But when a friend of ours faces the death of a partner, we must endeavor to be extremely compassionate and remember there is now a hole in that loved one's soul. The hole had been filled by her beloved, but now there is a void.

After a period of time has passed when a loved one has died, either expectedly or unexpectedly, it becomes necessary to do forgiveness work. One might ask, "What is there to forgive if I had only love for this person?" Yes, and now he's gone and you are left alone, perhaps with three kids to raise, perhaps with astronomical medical bills, perhaps with unmet expectations for your future with your loved one—a future that you must learn to navigate alone.

Forgiving your friend, parent, teacher, spouse for leaving is something we must all learn to do in time. Then it is necessary to forgive yourself for the difficulty and the struggle you are having or have had in releasing that loved one in order to go into the next level of your soul's journey.

The need and the opportunity to forgive shows up in virtually every level of living our lives. Forgiveness is a never-ending process. We may wish this wouldn't be so, but it is.

Whenever I feel stuck, even in a minute way, or I encounter people who are particularly annoying, I've learned to catch myself right away and ask: Who or what do I need to forgive? Whatever comes to mind I'll work on forgiving it, even if it seems irrelevant or silly. Thus, I forgave the congregant's daughters about the unpaid funeral bill until there was no bit of negative energy around the thought of them.

Forgiving in Paradise

We have moved to a remote area of Hawaii—Molokai. It is called the Friendly Isle for good reason: 99.9 percent of all encounters here have been positive. The one exception I've faced was in a new store in town that carried an interesting variety of goods not found elsewhere. I immediately began shopping there weekly for specialty items. One day after I had returned home and was unpacking bags, I realized that, instead of picking up a bottle of chardonnay, I had grabbed a bottle of sweet white wine that was not at all to my husband's and my liking.

A few days later I returned to the store to exchange the wine. As I placed the bottle on the counter, I explained my error to the owner. He gruffly pointed to the handwritten sign that read, *No Refunds*. I responded that I wasn't asking for a refund, I simply wanted to exchange the bottle for one of chardonnay. He said simply, "No refunds."

Puzzled, I asked, "Do you think this is a good policy?"

"Yes!" he snarled.

"Okay," I replied, becoming angry, "that may work for you, but it doesn't work for me. My shadow will never darken your door again." After saying that, I began to exit the store with the bottle I didn't want. But then I wheeled about, went back to the counter, put the wine down there, and said, "Here, you need this more than I do."

I was ticked off, angry, and I knew I needed to forgive him. It has been said that when we have a negative encounter, on average we will tell nineteen people. Well, I told five and felt guilty about that. I don't even know the owner's name. When seen spiritually, every grievance we hold can be likened to a day we encounter an unexpected teacher. He was mine, and he will never know it. I just know that if his unskilled behavior showed up in my life, it needed my attention. So I forgave him.

I have not had another negative encounter on Molokai since that one.

One of the lessons this experience taught me is that even in paradise there are crabby people, and we must forgive anyone whom we have allowed to disturb the calm peace of our soul. We always have the choice—grievance or serenity. Do we want to be right or happy? Sometimes our egos want to be "right," but our spirit always wants us to be happy.

We are forever making the decision between holding a grievance and experiencing a miracle. Every grievance we hold can be likened to a scrim—a translucent curtain—held before our eyes. Accumulate enough of them and they become an opaque drape, and we become blind to the spirit within us. Each thought and act of forgiveness lifts one of these scrims, slowly beginning to expose the light that has always been there but has been hidden.

This chapter begins with the story of the amazing monk Thich Quang Duc and ends with my annoyance at a store owner and his bottle of wine. Perhaps you think, How silly, how insignificant. But no. Every upset, big or small, is disturbing to our peace of mind. It is important that we realize this and be willing to heal *every* upset.

Hopefully none of us will have to take on the saintly task of forgiving a deranged boy who has murdered our family. The odds are far greater that someone will have dishonored you or discounted your worth or behaved in a very unconscious, unskilled manner. When scenarios similar to these present themselves in your life, train your mind stream through spiritual practice to turn away from revenge or anger and turn to forgiveness. When you practice doing so, you are traveling the highway to peace and happiness.

Make the detour into the light and leave the grievances behind in the dust of your past.

FORGIVENESS IN ACTION:
THE FORGIVENESS LETTER

Remember that I wrote a letter to the person I felt had disrespected me. I then safely burned the letter, allowing the flames to represent my letting go of the situation completely.

Now ask yourself if there is someone you are ready to forgive and if you're ready to let go of the hurt and anger you feel. Take a few deep breaths, and then write this person a letter. Express yourself fully and completely. At the end of the letter, state that you are now forgiving this person and letting go of the situation completely.

Finally, find a way to safely destroy this letter (please do this carefully!). As the letter is destroyed, keep breathing deeply and feel yourself letting the letter represent your willingness to let go of this person and this situation.

If in the future you feel upset or "charged" in any way by this situation, close your eyes for a few moments, take some breaths, and then see in your mind that letter and its contents being dissolved. Remind yourself that you've already done the hard work of letting go and are now choosing to be past the situation. If you still find yourself emotionally connected to the hurt, write another letter and follow the process again. Don't judge yourself during this process. Sometimes it takes several letters before we feel completely able to let go and forgive and be free.

CHAPTER 2

Forgiveness Points the Way

*We must develop and maintain the capacity to
forgive. He who is devoid of the power to
forgive is devoid of the power to love.*

—MARTIN LUTHER KING, JR.

Why forgive? A simple, succinct answer is provided
in *A Course in Miracles*: "Forgiveness offers everything I want." It's to the point . . . and yet so hard for
people to get. A frustrated student of mine exclaimed,
"You don't understand! I want it all!" To which I responded, "You'd better get busy."

The way to freedom and liberation has been taught
and pointed out for millennia. In the Christian Gospels
there is a story of Jesus's cousin John the Baptist report-
ing that a great being was coming. As a matter of fact he
was so great that John wasn't even worthy of fastening
his sandals.

John had appeared in the desert area of the wilderness proclaiming baptism and forgiveness, teaching the lesson of cleansing for one to be washed clean. The locals flocked to John. When I think of that first-century scene through the lens of a twenty-first-century woman, I wonder, "Just what was going on in town?"

John supposedly was a wild-looking man wearing animal skins, and probably quite unkempt, proclaiming one much more powerful than he would soon be coming.

Once a longtime friend of mine, Amy, had a much-younger boyfriend—emphasis on "boy." He had to be twenty years younger than her. George was wild, woolly, and seemed to me to be a bit deranged. My friend's radar for picking men had long been out of focus and broken. Whenever I saw him, which was seldom, the thought would cross my mind that he was taking on more and more of the persona of John the Baptist.

My friend finally gave this young man the boot and I thought, "Thank God." After several years had passed, he began showing up at every West Coast event featuring the Dalai Lama that I attended. He began to look more wild and woolly and to act even more strangely. For instance, he had taken to wearing nothing but untanned animal skins tied with a clothesline rope around his waist. Fortunately for me he no longer recognized me (or much else).

He would boldly walk past the heavy security, straight down the middle aisle, and start looking for a seat in the "sponsor" section all the way in the front. Security was always close behind, and together they would gather up George and quietly exit the arena. When I told my companions that I knew that guy, they would in unison raise their eyebrows and look at me like I was the crazy one. Then he would come again, this time down a side aisle, with security close on his heels, and the whole exit scene would be repeated.

My heart went out to George. He appeared to be such a lost soul. After prayerful consideration I decided not to tell Amy (his former gal pal) that he had begun showing up at the Dalai Lama presentations or of his unusual demeanor. Years had passed since they'd lived together, and during that time my friend had done much forgiveness work on herself and him, focusing on several issues:

- Why had she once again chosen an inappropriate partner?
- What in herself was she not dealing with that led her instead to find wounded men to rescue?
- How was this activity keeping her from her real purpose?

I told no one I had begun spotting him except my husband and a close mutual friend. Then the phone call came from our mutual friend that this disturbed soul had killed himself.

The mutual friend felt very strongly that, in order to have peace, Amy needed to know what I knew. Reluctantly I made the phone call and shared what I had witnessed. Amazingly, Amy told me even more bizarre details of his life. Among other things, George had claimed to head up a secret security force for the Dalai Lama. I shook my head silently in disbelief. I truly knew his tales had come out of his delusional mind and everything he'd related had never happened. I just kept saying to myself: It never happened; it never happened—and to her it never happened.

George had been a troubled, lost individual, and Amy finally extricated herself from this very unhealthy relationship. She did it by faithfully engaging in her spiritual practices, particularly forgiveness, in order to remove from her conscious and subconscious mind all the complicated aspects of dysfunction. She repeated this simple yet powerful affirmation again and again, affirming it, writing it, meditating on it:

"George, I forgive you, I release you, I let you go. All cords that have bound us together are now dissolved. We are both at peace now and forever."

She became at peace in the now, and George is at peace in the hereafter.

Amy then spent several years alone to make certain she had healed herself to the depths. Now she is finally in a balanced, loving relationship with a kind, considerate, emotionally healthy man. And for the first time in the thirty years that I have known her, she is peaceful and happy. Forgiveness helped Amy to heal her past and cleanse herself of past beliefs and behaviors, so she could be ready for a loving relationship.

Let the teaching "Forgiveness offers everything I want" continue to arise in your consciousness. I know that the work each one of us does on forgiveness is almost never ending.

Forgiving the Family

Amy is no spiritual lightweight, and her story of the power of forgiveness didn't end with George. In fact, the experience with George helped her to go even deeper in her forgiveness work. Amy is deeply committed to working on herself and is very aware that the abuse she suffered as a child was raging in her and manifesting as dysfunction. Like too many children, she was raised by extremely wounded and cruel parents. They were active members of a religious cult that advocated "spare the rod and spoil the child." There was no sparing the rod in this stoic New England family. There was no sexual abuse, but her young body bore the welts and scars of merciless beatings and burnings. It is painful for me to recall the miserable facts of her childhood.

A gifted musician, Amy gains solace from song. At an early age she began to sing at church gatherings and revivals. Her adult voice is crystal clear. People often comment that she sings like an angel . . . and she does. In recent years she has learned to use her voice as an instrument for healing, as she invokes soft tones to go into her heart or her hands and assist others in their own healing process. This is the same heart, the same hands that were damaged by both mother and father. This trauma had embedded itself in the very cells of her being.

Over the years Amy has literally embraced every forgiveness technique she and I have ever known. In order to be free she distanced herself from her parents for decades, though she would send them holiday and birthday cards, and she invited them to every significant occasion in her life, including college graduation. But they never came. Never. Yet she continued daily to work on forgiving them.

Not long ago Amy received an e-mail from her estranged sister informing her that their father had advanced Alzheimer's disease and had been placed in a nursing facility by their mother. The unexpected e-mail closed with the line, "Just thought you'd want to know."

That was it. Amy immediately made plans to travel across the country to see her parents. If her mother chose not to see her, that was her choice, but nothing would stop her from going. Shortly before leaving, she spoke warmly of her mother to me. Right before Amy left she called her mother, and—in a compassionate moment—her mother warned her that she might be in for a shock when she saw her father. For he had stopped speaking several weeks before, and at this stage he recognized no one. Amy responded, "That's okay. I'll recognize him."

On the long flight from the West to the East Coast she prayed without ceasing. She spent the first night in a bed-and-breakfast she had booked for three nights. Early the next morning she drove around her hometown of long ago. Then she knew it was time to begin her mission and her reason for being there.

When Amy arrived at the nursing home, she was told that her mother was in her father's room. When she reached the room, he was in his wheelchair just outside in the hall with a number of his "neighbors," all staring blankly at nothing in particular. When she spotted her father, he looked up and in a loud, clear voice said, "Looky, looky, looky, look who's here!"

Tears rolled down Amy's cheeks as she reached down and held him—a wizened, feeble old man who had traumatized her childhood. As she continued to embrace him, any remaining cellular trauma melted out of her.

When she released her embrace she saw her mother, now elderly and feeble herself, standing in the doorway taking it all in and crying as well. Amy moved toward her mother and extended her arms for a hug for the first time in over twenty-five years. What followed caused Amy nearly to faint as her knees buckled. Her mother said, "Can you ever forgive me—us—for all the pain we caused you?"

Amy responded, "I already have, or I wouldn't be here now."

The three of them went into her father's room, where Amy began to sing a healing song. She later reported that both her parents began to relax and then fell asleep while holding hands. It was the first time she'd ever seen her parents be affectionate with one another. She had never seen her parents hold hands as she was growing up. This same warm scene was repeated the next two mornings, and when it was time for Amy to leave she held them both, saying good-bye forever.

When she drove back to the airport, she felt a wondrous relief that was indescribable. That feeling continued as she boarded her flight and flew back to the West Coast.

It is a precious gift to arrive at such a place of forgiveness and completion after decades dedicated to becoming totally free from the past and healed of it. Since that deeply personal experience of using her voice as a healing instrument, Amy has been able to support her clients on a whole new level of soul healing. She is now an authority on soul matters.

By so deeply and completely forgiving her parents and

allowing the past to dissolve, Amy can now finally embrace her innocence and holiness. It is an incredible outworking of life to witness. The years she spent forgiving and healing her deep wounds from the past was the *only* way she could restore her mental health.

Did she wait for them to ask for forgiveness? No.

Did she wait for one or both of her parents to say, "I'm sorry"? No.

She forgave them not because they deserved to be forgiven but because *she deserved to live free from the trauma of her past*. Through her years of doing forgiveness work, she has prepared herself for her own enlightenment.

My father's youngest brother is seventeen years younger than my dad. Uncle Mike is a quiet, unassuming man who has raised, mostly on his own, a brood of children—ten, to be exact. As I grew up, I witnessed how devoted he was to each one of his offspring. Sadly, two of his children drowned, on separate occasions. That left him with six boys and two girls.

Mike was a noble father, raising bright, well-mannered, well-groomed children. They were all polite and would look adults in the eye when they spoke to them, although remaining very respectful to their elders.

Mike loved his kids and it showed. If any two of them

would get into an argument or a scuffle with each other, he would sit them down and give them a talking-to. In essence he would say: You can argue with the whole world when you grow up, but you are not leaving this room until you make peace with each other. In other words: Forgive each other now.

Today they are all grown up, most with families of their own. They get along well and share lots of love with one another. How they live their lives is admirable.

So many families are at war within their own family unit. My mom and her only sister did not speak for thirty years. Thirty years! What a waste of almost half a lifetime. Thank goodness they eventually forgave each other in their later years and developed a close bond once again.

The Dalai Lama teaches that we need to make amends with our adversary, because one day everyone involved will be dead. My mom and aunt are both dead, and thank God they made amends and do not have to carry with them what the Buddhists call "a polluted mind stream" on their souls' journeys.

Diana Ross's daughter Tracee—now a popular actress in her own right—speaking on a TV talk show, told how, if she and a sibling were at odds with each other, their mother would put them in a room together and say, "Don't come out until you can sincerely say, 'I'm sorry. I love you.'" If they came out of the room and repeated,

"I'm sorry. I love you," without much sincerity, their mother would not be convinced and would send them back into the room until they could come out and really mean what they were saying.

With loving parental upbringing such as my uncle Mike and Diana Ross exhibited, peace and harmony would always prevail. There would be space to work out any anger and animosity. I know of legions of families where this was not the case, where adult siblings barely tolerate one another at best or—like my mother and aunt—don't speak for decades.

If you are in such a family situation, come to resolution now. Make amends now. Forgive now. Be the one to extend the olive branch. Even if peace doesn't come to the other person involved in the separating experience, it will come to your heart and mind.

Unforgiveness Harms You

When we can begin to view forgiveness as the spiritual act we must do for ourselves, then we may be willing to forgive. And we need to forgive others in order to be free.

Here is a startling news flash for some: The unforgiving thoughts, the resentful thoughts, the pile of grievances you line up against another person do nothing to hurt that individual. Your unwillingness to forgive is not doing any harm to that person. But it is certainly harming you. Your grievances are blocking your future happiness, your future good. Remember, every grievance hurts you and not the other person. He or she may not even remember your name, let alone the situation that was the catalyst for your animosity.

Freedom from Victimhood

Think of being unforgiving and holding on to a grievance as actually attacking yourself and keeping yourself in victim consciousness.

Barry was always mercilessly teased and bullied by his older brother Hank. The mean, unkind brother had the clear signs of a budding sociopath. He tormented and emotionally tortured Barry, who did not forgive him and instead carried Hank around in his head every day of his unhappy life. Even though Hank was no longer in his life, Barry continued to be the victim of Hank's cruelty as he frequently replayed childhood events and reignited his own anger over and over. Barry's victimhood was no different at forty from how it was when he was eight.

For Barry to have a future different from his pain-filled childhood it was crucial that he forgive his brother, whom he hadn't seen in over a decade. Barry had to see the necessity of forgiving Hank for his own sake, under-standing it had nothing to do with Hank.

Barry began saying a very powerful affirmation:

I am never the victim of anyone in my world.

Barry worked with this statement of truth, writing it over and over and over in his journal in order to begin healing his soul.

I have taught many to use this affirmation, and varia-tions of it, and on occasion I still use it myself. It may take several days or weeks, or perhaps even longer, but eventually it begins to reach the subconscious pain and turn it around.

Try writing that affirmation down for yourself. After each writing, pause for a moment and reflect on your inner feelings, paying attention to anything uncomfort-able that begins to arise.

Barry wrote:

- *I am never the victim of anyone in my world.*
- *I am no longer the victim of Hank.*
- *Hank no longer has control over me.*

What first arose in Barry was: *I'll always be Hank's punching bag. I hate Hank. He is a mean, cruel bastard.*

Then Barry returned to his affirmations:

- *I am never the victim of anyone in my world.*
- *I am no longer the victim of Hank.*
- *Hank no longer has control over me.*

Barry thought: *God! The very thought of him and how he tortured me makes me nauseated.*

This process was very painful for Barry, but he vowed to continue on. He had so much to regurgitate that it took him several months of dedicated forgiveness practice before the energy began to shift. It was after doing this forgiveness work that Barry noticed his chronic gastrointestinal problems were beginning to ease. He found he was resting better and experiencing less free-floating anxiety. His thoughts were quieting down and the incessant monkey mind-chatter was finally shutting up. Today Barry believes that the power of forgiveness healed his mind and also helped to heal his body.

At last the cords that had bound him to his sociopathic brother were severed. Now he was free to link up with kind and caring people and strong enough never to draw another Hank into his life. Forgiveness had freed Barry from his self-constructed prison. He could at long last embrace for himself the phrase Martin Luther King, Jr., made famous: "Free at last, free at last, thank God Almighty, we are free at last."

I have long taught that forgiveness is the gift we give ourselves. Do you want a quiet heart, peace of mind, freedom from anxiety, a calm countenance, a healthy body, joy in your heart? All this and so much more is what forgiveness offers you.

Why do people insist on holding on to the pain? Perhaps because it's familiar; perhaps because it's a habit; perhaps because the person has yet to consider there could be a way out. What would life be like without the familiar goblins? What would shape the person's thoughts, words, and actions?

No matter what the circumstances or events, there is always a way out. No matter what. Nothing is too horrific that grace cannot enter and heal. Peace can be restored to your restless, sometimes tortured, mind.

In a very concrete sense, forgiveness can lead one to seek out the best healing modality, the right therapist or therapy, so that whatever complementary healing work that needs to be done can be done.

Forgiveness gives one the courage to do the necessary work in order to be free. Forgiveness allows us to look at our pain and not freeze in it or drown in it, but begin to realign our lives and process the hurt. If we keep on keeping on we eventually begin to be set free and move out of victim consciousness.

The joy, the release that comes, cannot be described with words. Life truly does transform. Everything in the outer sphere may look the same, but nothing feels the same. From time to time I still see a bumper sticker from years back: *Shift happens*—a reversal of meaning from the original, negative, scatological bumper sticker. When we are willing to do the work and be committed to it, a shift in consciousness does happen.

What does it mean when you experience a shift in consciousness? You get to be happy. You get to be free. You get to create a new, bright and shining future.

No person or circumstance is deserving of your freedom but you; so if you have ever given your freedom away, take it back and take it back now!

Forgiving as Compassion

When I was young and naïve and lacking wisdom, I thought a certain male friend, whom I later married, held all my good. I couldn't be happy unless he loved me. I wasn't valuable unless he thought I was valuable. My sense of self-worth was all entwined with his ego. Thirty-five years ago I attended the workshop of a very popular newspaper columnist of the time, Sydney J. Harris. I don't remember much of the contents of this workshop, but I have never forgotten one profound thing he said:

"Theirs was a marriage made in heaven. The rocks in his head fit perfectly with the holes in her head."

Yep. That was me. It took a mountain of work to forgive myself. I needed to forgive myself even more than my ex-husband, because I had so willingly walked into that relationship and stayed.

When I look back and reflect on that time, it's as though I'm talking about someone else. That girl of so long ago is so much not who I became or who I am today. But I needed the fodder for my soul, and I surely created the drama so I would get my fair share of grist for my mill. I was an ignorant girl who married an ignorant boy. Neither one of us was mature enough to go steady, let alone be married.

He came from a family that was more dysfunctional than most. His father was a business executive who was highly educated and sophisticated. His mother was not. She was from the South, and as my college roommate would say at the time, "In her mind she lived at Tara from *Gone with the Wind.*"

Today I can see that this poor soul was severely mentally ill. At the time I thought she was stark, raving mad. She was paranoid and thought various people were spying on her. Once, when my then boyfriend and I were walking out of the living room, I dropped a hanky on the floor. His mother went ballistic, claiming that the motion was part of a secret code. When he and I were married a couple of years later, his mother attempted to French kiss all of the groomsmen. It was not only embarrassing to me, it was icky.

This elephant in the living room was enormous, and

although she was a frequent "visitor" to several psych wards, no one would face what was going on right under their noses.

Fast-forward several years to when I was filing for divorce. My dear mother said to me, "I hope you aren't getting a divorce because of his family and especially his mother."

"No, I'm not," I responded. "But it sure will be a nice benefit to no longer have to deal with her." And it was. However, at the time I had no idea how much forgiveness work I needed to do with regard to my ex-husband and his family, especially his mother. As I began to awaken spiritually, I began the necessary forgiveness work.

Through forgiveness I could see him as the innocent child who was raised in a household that never looked at or acknowledged any problem. When I saw him as the victim of his circumstances and upbringing, that alone made it so much easier to forgive him. Then I could begin to forgive his mother. When I was so young it was very difficult for me to have much understanding; that didn't come about until much maturity and spiritual insight had settled in.

After a long, long time I began to see his mother through the eyes of compassion and understanding. She was not exhibiting such bizarre behaviors to torture her son's bride, but rather because she was mentally ill.

Back then I did not have much knowledge of boundaries—what they are and how necessary they are. In dealing with a difficult individual like this, a spiritually mature person would:

- Limit contact.
- Always have at least one other person present during any less-than-pleasant interaction.
- Agree with the adversary quickly, as Jesus taught.
- Not take anything that happens personally.
- Turn the other cheek.
- Not gossip about the person or situation.
- Practice loving-kindness.
- Practice having a generous spirit.
- Practice forgiving until you can succeed with all of the above.

The Golden Key Method

An old yet effective technique is called "the Golden Key," a spiritual practice created by early-twentieth-century spiritual leader Emmet Fox. Instead of thinking endlessly about what is troubling you, think instead about God. You can choose to think about Mother Mary or Jesus or any deity with whom you identify. I use the Holy Spirit.

Put your faith in the object of your Golden Key and allow nothing to disturb the calm peace of your holy mind. If at nineteen I had realized my mind was holy and I could actually think thoughts with God, then I would have instantly ceased from polluting my mind stream and instead subdued all negative thoughts through spiritual practices. Thus, I would have been released so much earlier from my self-made prison.

Early Release

The high school on Molokai in Hawaii has a huge banner out front of the building that reads, *Early Release*. I've driven past that banner many times, and each time I chuckle as if it's the first time. What would it look like for you if you could have early release from your pain, suffering, negative mind stream, and hurtful karma?

Just before sitting down to write this chapter, I watched a friend's sermon through online streaming. What is remarkable about this man, among many things, is that he has stage 4 cancer. He spoke on quantum physics and asked his congregation to imagine what it would look like to reinvent our past. What if both the beautiful and the painful events had never occurred?

It's a difficult concept to wrap our brains around.

Certainly it causes us to think outside the box of our normal, everyday consciousness. If your past had never happened, who would you be today? Who would you be if you didn't have that history to weigh you down?

Here's an exercise: Place two chairs facing each other in a room where you will not be disturbed. Sit down in one and imagine your younger self entering the room and sitting across from you.

Ask your younger self, "How's it going? Tell me. Are you happy? Are you having fun? Is your life meaningful? Do you feel your life matters at this point? I will listen. Please talk to me." Then be still and listen. Take notes. Get to know your undamaged self.

I once had a client named Nancy do this exercise in a counseling appointment. The first time all she could do was cry. She felt so unwanted and so unloved by her self-consumed mother and absent father. We ended the session and picked it up one week later. She sobbed again, but she spoke, saying, "I am a good little girl. I am."

I held her as she continued to cry. It seemed like she had an ocean of uncried tears locked inside. She felt unloved and unlovable at her core. To think of having a happy childhood was about as difficult as thinking of flying to Jupiter.

"I want you to talk to that wounded little Nancy," I instructed. "Tell her she is and was innocent. Tell her she is and was lovable. Love her now. Stop seeing her painful past. You are upset today because you live out of thirty-year-old energy. That energy is gone. It's alive only because you keep it alive. When you look in the mirror, you see only the past. The lenses you wear show you only that old, painful history."

To engage a quantum physics approach in our lives we must reorchestrate everything we have believed to be true about time. We must engage new and different ideas about time.

I told Nancy that the past she saw was so vile that everything currently looks vile as well. "You think you are seeing the world as it truly is. You are not. Because you view your mother and father as enemies, you now subconsciously view everyone as an enemy."

To permanently change our view of the world for the better takes a lot of work, but Nancy and all of us are up to the task. In time we can all learn to take all the emotional charge out of the past. Then the day will come when forgiveness is so complete that we will have no past. We will have no enemies. And we will have compassion for our parents and everyone we have thought to have injured us.

Nancy can become a holy person. We all can become holy, blessing everyone. The past will no longer contain a person filled with holes.

FORGIVENESS IN ACTION:
AFFIRMATIONS FOR FORGIVING

Affirmations can be powerful tools to unlock our blocks to forgiving ourselves and/or forgiving others. Try using the following affirmations in two ways: written and spoken aloud. Begin by getting a journal, then find a comfortable place to sit, where you won't be disturbed for a while. Take a few deep breaths to ground yourself. Think about the person who you feel wronged you, who you want to forgive. Keep breathing deeply as you then begin to write down the following affirmations in your journal:

I forgive you, I release you, I let you go. All cords that have bound us together are now dissolved. We are both at peace now and forever.

Write it at least seventy times in your journal. As you write it in your journal, say it aloud as well. This will help you to keep your mind and your body focused on the same activity. Do this again every day for at least a week. At the end of the week, before writing the affirmations, stop and notice if you feel any different now. Do you have the same level of anger or sadness or ill will? Did you experience any changes in the course of the week that might be a result of your letting-go process? Can you see the signs of forgiveness happening? If you feel like this completes your forgiveness process, then bless it and stop. If you still feel upset and that more forgiveness needs to happen, then begin writing the affirmation seventy times again each day for the next seven days, and then reevaluate. Take as long as you need until you feel the forgiveness happen.

You can also think of other affirmations that may help, to add or replace the ones above. For instance, if you are feeling like someone else victimized you, then write:

I am never the victim of anyone in my world.

Be creative, and find the affirmation or affirmations that will take you out of being a victim and into being forgiveness in action.

CHAPTER 3

Calling All Helpers

All the effort must be made by you.
Buddha only shows the way.

—THE BUDDHA

received a phone call from a woman from my past who was very upset with God. Rather than being annoyed with her, I silently thanked her because she triggered an entire stream of consciousness in me.

This woman saw God as a fairy godmother, Santa Claus, and the boogeyman all morphed into one. It seems that a year previous she had set a course for herself in which she would follow what she perceived as the most important spiritual "rules." She would (1) pray for fifteen minutes a day; (2) meditate twice a day; (3) forgive anyone with whom she had issues (I pointed out that she still sounded quite angry); (4) tithe to her church for one year;

(5) cease from gossiping; (6) do kind acts; and (7) read uplifting material.

After one year, she told me, her life was not better and she had quit doing it all. There. It was settled. God did not work in her life, and she was done with God. She was angry, continuously upset, and very, very naïve.

She kept saying to me, "I did all this for one year! I did not gossip for one year. Do you have any idea how hard that was? And my life got worse!" I have to admit that I found her whining incredibly immature.

She waxed on endlessly about how it all didn't work, until I told her to cease. I said there was nothing I could do for her if she wanted to bitch and moan and say how the spirit does not work. She would have to find another pair of ears, because mine had heard enough.

She exclaimed once again, "But I did all this for one whole year!"

I responded, "I've done all that and more for forty years and I never received a medal."

A line full of wisdom that my dear cousin Joe uses flooded my consciousness. When something huge and horrible happens in our lives, we talk about it and tell everyone. Joe succinctly explains, "First, it's sad. Second, it's tragic. Third, it's boring." She needed to quit talking about it. She needed to quit being such a victim. Her story had become boring.

We practice living a spiritual life because we know

that it is the only choice to make—not because we are bartering with and testing God.

She was thinking like a child and behaving like a child. A number of years ago I learned from a brilliant psychiatrist that most people are babies clothed in adult bodies. Her work, she claimed, was a bit of Freud and a large portion of herself, Dr. Judith Alexander.

When she first taught me this in her office I was attempting to deal with a number of very difficult personalities. Very calmly she stated: "People are babies."

"Yes, Judith, I know. People can be incredibly immature," I said, thinking I understood what she was saying. To which she leaned forward and yelled at me, "People are babies!" She then proceeded to rattle off a half dozen examples of extremely immature and narcissistic acts appearing at that time in the news.

She continued: "Adults do not kill their own children. Adults do not abuse their children. Adults do not go to the school, mall, or theater and shoot innocent victims randomly. Adults do not attempt to drown their problems with alcohol or drugs."

Judith was on a roll, and she kept rolling by giving example after example. Then she abruptly stopped and yelled again, "People are babies!"

I got it! Just because someone is older does not in any way, shape, or form mean they have grown into an adult or are any wiser.

Said Judith, "I have not sat in this chair for twenty-eight years without learning a thing or two."

That one hour with her and that lesson have had an enormous impact on my life from that moment to this. She later explained that, generally speaking, there are very few true adults on the planet. Most people cease from truly maturing emotionally after the ages of two to four. Yes, two to four years of age is where most people stop growing "up" and grow "sideways" instead. While I'm simplifying what she taught, she explained that her conclusions had come from a very complex and in-depth study into the human psyche, one beyond my ability to completely explain. But the kernel of what she was teaching me felt absolutely true.

Judith told me that if she could get a patient in therapy who was stuck as a toddler of two to progress to the age of four, her work was done. Or if the patient started at four and progressed to six, her work was done. She would then release these patients from her care.

When we have the insight that the person who hurt us was not acting out of his or her adult self but out of his or her two-year-old self, our forgiveness road becomes a lot less bumpy.

A two-year-old might, for example, throw a temper tantrum because he wants to nurse. If the mother accedes to his tantrum, he may bite her nipple rather than suckle it. When the same little boy grows up stuck at that age, as a thirty-seven-year-old, he may yell and attack and scream, "I hate you!" in the same childlike attempt to get more attention. Or he may use a "grown-up" version of a tantrum, such as making manipulative comments that undermine or demean.

Why is this important? When we realize that some of the people who attack or hurt us are behaving unconsciously from their unmatured psyche, then it helps us to find compassion, which in turns helps us to forgive. We may even get a window into our own level of maturity, and find opportunities to mature emotionally ourselves, and to forgive ourselves. If someone in your life is acting like an adult child, then stop for a moment, remember he or she is acting from that unhealed place, and then release the person. Don't attempt to be the parent; rather, call on your inner adult to forgive and walk away.

Finding a Divine Mentor

We all need a spiritual mentor, someone to help us monitor our progress, a helper to hold a beacon before us to illuminate the way. This can be someone who is alive and you have access to, or it can be someone from history or sacred texts, whose life and words inspire you to new realms of understanding and experience. Meditate to discover who you are drawn to for your spiritual guidance.

Here are some suggestions to get your wheels turning in that direction:

- A patriarch or noble character from the Bible—one who embodies qualities you admire or would like to emulate.
- If you come from a Christian background, you could choose Jesus, Mother Mary, or one of the apostles. For instance, if you need more faith, you'd choose Peter. For greater experiences of love, you'd choose John.
- Maybe you're drawn to Moses, and you need to embody greater commitment to an unwavering ideal.
- Or you may choose a spiritual leader, perhaps outside your religious tradition, like the Buddha, Krishna, Sri Yukteswar, Gandhi, Mother Meera, Sai Baba, Joan of Arc, or your own legendary ancestor.

After you decide on the one, meditate on this subject and you'll know. Ask that the essence of that holy one be with you and guide you in your earthly and spiritual endeavors.

You are not wedded to this sage for all of eternity and may ask for assistance from different ones under a variety of circumstances—such as a woman in childbirth or having female difficulties calling on Mary for guidance and comfort.

Working with our divine helpers needs our attention for a lifetime. Unless we have attained complete spiritual enlightenment (and I know no one who has achieved that), we will still have grievances against others. When we hold a grievance against another person, we have forgotten who we are. In such a situation we play small, and in our role of playacting we take on the role of victim. We falsely believe some other person has done something dastardly toward us. Once again we are making the choice to let the ego rule the mind. Therefore, we are not in our right mind.

Holding a grievance splits us off from our divine self, from our compassion, from our holiness. As difficult as it may seem to be in some situations, forgiveness always has a place in our minds. But if we are to know peace and our troubled mind is to find rest and remember who we are, forgiveness is essential. When we ask for help from our mentor, we can begin to see clearly, begin to let go and forgive.

Getting Unstuck from Our Grievances

When people come to me who are extremely stuck in their particular grievance, their own personal hell, I do my very best to compassionately listen. While one part of my brain is listening and evaluating, the other part of my brain will wonder if the individual is willing to let this particular upset go and allow peace to take its place. Too often the answer is: "No, this person is not."

A close friend has become a master at making herself miserable. She is a very successful self-made woman who stopped maturing at about age sixteen, when she immersed herself in her quest to go into medicine. A driven woman, she succeeded. The only child of immigrant parents who had died by the time she was a freshman in college, she carried on alone with dogged determination.

By the time she graduated from medical school at the top of her class, she was known as Snow White, the beautiful brainiac with alabaster skin and raven black hair. She was accepted into a top-ranked hospital for her internship, continuing to shine with her skills. But socially she remained a teenager (à la Dr. Judith's theory)—actually, much younger than that.

The years passed. After two marriages and two divorces, one son, and several moves around the country as she continued to thrive professionally, one Sunday she walked into my church with a doctor friend whom I knew slightly. They were dating.

At church they clung together like teenagers. He looked at her like he could eat her with a spoon for lunch.

She and I, as two professional women, became friends. She was European and exuded that old-world charm. Soon she and her boyfriend were making plans for an elaborate destination wedding, and she asked me to be the offici- ant. I happily agreed.

The wedding was elegant and beautiful, with over one hundred friends making the journey to share in the cele- bration. Several of her physician colleagues said to me that they thought she was finally going to be happy.

Unfortunately that happiness was short-lived. Al- though they both shared the same medical specialty, each began to second-guess the other and found many petty things to complain about:

- His complaint: She would call to him from an- other room and start talking before joining him in the same room.
- Her complaint: He would leave uncashed checks from his speaking fees lying all over his home office (over $50,000 worth).
- His complaint: He saw her neatness as excessive.
- Her complaint: She no longer thought his ab- sentminded professor style was charming.

And on and on and on the grievances went.
Finally they came to me for marital counseling, which

for me was a nightmare. After a few sessions I told them I could no longer counsel them. He knew he was right. She knew she was right. Neither would give an inch. Their bickering like teenagers was counterproductive for them and exhausting for me.

If there was any hope for their future, at least one of them would have to decide to grow up. I have always seen that being right at all costs means sacrificing happiness. They each had to be right, thus eliminating happiness as a possibility. This continual need to be right eventually led to their divorce.

My friend is brilliant in many ways, but sometimes she behaves like an emotional cripple. A short time after the divorce, she took me as a guest to London with her. As soon as the plane lifted off, she began obsessing about her ex. "Please," I pleaded, "let us not take him across the Atlantic with us." Her obsessing continued long after our London trip.

My attempts to coach her on forgiveness and the need to forgive him fell on deaf ears. She hasn't forgiven him or even made the slightest attempt to do so. Nor has she looked at the need to forgive herself. Several years have passed, and my dear friend continues to make herself sick over that long-dead relationship. It is truly sad to see her stuck in this way (not to mention boring to keep hearing the same complaints!).

Remember, I've learned that some psychologists explain that the energy from an actual event lasts about ninety seconds. If we hold on to it beyond that time, it is because we make the effort to keep it mentally and emotionally alive. To do so takes a lot of energy. It is a total and complete waste of the hours, weeks, days, and years of your precious life to keep a negative memory or experience alive.

My friend could experience such freedom and joy if she would only channel her brilliance into creating the life she says she truly wants by quitting her incessant stirring up of unhappy, negative energy from the past.

She is simply not ready to alter her dusty script, so each day she reawakens her pain. And it visits her like the first time every time. It is a miserable way to live. As brilliant as she is intellectually, she is just as underdeveloped emotionally. She is, as Dr. Judith taught, an immature child who keeps hurting herself.

The scope of her life could be so much broader, but her myopic vision will not allow her unhealed self to see the bigger picture.

Eventually I found myself avoiding this friend and no longer wanted to travel abroad with her. Those supposedly free trips, where she paid my way, began to cost me a lot in terms of attention, time, patience, and emotional energy. It seemed like I had my own forgiveness work to do with her! I sat down to meditate on how to release my judgment and irritation with this friend.

I decided that the forgiveness work that I could do for her, as her friend and minister, was to:

1. Pray for her and her ex.
2. Never engage with her in conversation about her past.
3. Allow her the freedom to stay in her misery until she's had enough. I'll still be there for her when she's ready to move on.

This allowed me to see her in a whole new and compassionate light. It also allowed me to create healthy boundaries in our friendship, which has helped us both experience each other more positively. For our souls to attain peace and lasting freedom, we absolutely must realize that forgiveness is the only way out of our self-built prisons.

Every Day in Every Way

Sometimes returning to the teachings of the past can be helpful. Émile Coué was one of the earliest leaders in modern metaphysical thought. He created what many regard as the first affirmation:

*Every day in every way I am getting better and
better.*

You can substitute much in the affirmation to fit your
particular needs. For instance:

*Every day in every way I am getting happier and
happier.*
*Every day in every way I am getting healthier and
healthier.*
*Every day in every way I am forgiving and letting
go of all thoughts that hurt.*

Repetitive use of an affirmation both said aloud and
written can begin to alter your old, stuck programming
and begin to introduce new pathways of positive change.

Self-forgiveness

Whitney Houston famously sang that loving yourself is
"the greatest love of all." There is much truth in these
words, but Whitney lived the plight of the common woman
or man. She couldn't or hadn't learned to live her song.

This is not uncommon. The philosopher who does not
always live up to his philosophy. The therapist who does
not live up to his knowledge and is an active alcoholic.

The minister who is a skirt chaser. On and on the list goes. In one way or another we have all fallen short of the ideal.

When we grow—if we are to grow at all—we must learn to practice forgiving ourselves until our destructive behaviors change and are eliminated, transformed. Then what we express must be in alignment with how we are living our lives, and our actions must match our words. They both reflect the inner essence of our being.

The breadth and height of your transgressions will give you a fair evaluation of the extent of the forgiveness work you need to be doing on yourself. When you forgive, you are releasing yourself from illusions, from all the falsehoods you have convinced yourself are real. You then achieve freedom, and the release is incredibly uplifting and almost indescribable.

- You breathe more deeply.
- You rest in quiet, refreshing sleep.
- You laugh more quickly.
- You enjoy life more.

Richard Levy, a spiritual brother of mine, dealt with advanced cancer in the most enlightened way I have ever witnessed. His funny bone expanded to embrace all of his bones. He appeared to be finding joy in everything. He harbored no grievances as a result of this disease. He lived each day to the fullest and lived it in joy. When he laughed, his compact frame seemed to be expanding in every direction. His mirth bubbled up from his depths.

He appeared as a "fool for God," as the Sufis taught so long ago. He knew he was dying, and he had actually gotten the cosmic joke. He became a shape-shifter, effortlessly slipping between the realms of consciousness.

Richard demonstrated to all who knew and loved him that his approaching death was not real. His body was passing away, but he knew he was not dying. He knew he was oh so much more than his body, so he laughed at the absurdity of the drama all the way to his physical end.

I was impressed.

Richard was one of four people with whom I feel quite spiritually close who are or were experiencing raging cancers. Three of them clearly walk the spiritual path and have made it their mission to continue doing so even in the face of the most grim of diagnoses. One abandoned his spiritual life years ago and has lived mostly in rage from that moment until now.

The first two, a woman and a man, are using their experiences for their enlightenment. What I have to offer these precious ones—who have helped countless people awaken, heal, grow, learn to love, and be happy—is my very focused prayers and a gentle reminder to keep on forgiving themselves, even if they believe they have forgiven everything and everyone they could.

For the fourth all I can do is pray for him. He believes that how I live and what I teach is poppycock. Obviously I have no need to go to his level and make myself as miserable as he is. So I pray and forgive, pray and forgive.

The first man I'm talking about wrote to his family and friends: "The doctor says the cancer has invaded other areas and shows no signs of slowing down. There are no other options available." So what has he done? He's fallen more deeply in love with life, he's fastened his seat belt, and he is enjoying the ride.

How much time do these three have left to enjoy the ride? Who can say? Richard has already left. It appears that at least two of the others are on their way to enlightenment, and this disease is their train ticket (rocket ticket?) there. Their end date for this incarnation approaches.

At such a time, the more conscious among us think: Okay, it's now or never. If I'm leaving soon let me leave consciously. If I have anything or anyone to forgive, let me do it now.

I know a middle-aged woman who got the most disheartening diagnosis from her physician that her end date was near. She was devastated. A close friend suggested that she see a great spiritual teacher from India who would soon be visiting their town and teaching his philosophy.

Eastern philosophies were not her cup of tea, but she was desperate with fear so she went. There was a large crowd, so she waited until the man had finished speaking in order to have a quiet word with him. She stood before him respectfully and tried to speak, but she burst into tears instead.

The guru looked at her and with great compassion asked, "My dear, whatever is the matter?"

"I'm dying," she choked out between tears. "I'm dying."

He threw his head back and roared with laughter. "You're dying, my dear? Why, we are all dying!"

That was the precise moment of her awakening. She got it. That night for the first time she stepped onto her spiritual path, and perhaps it's no surprise that she is still very much alive. She is fulfilled and happy and engaged with life as she had never been before.

If you long to awaken, do it now. If you need to forgive yourself or anyone or anything, do it now. If you want to be unshackled, take off your self-made chains now. Be free now. Do your spiritual practice now. Do not wait until the angel of death is knocking on your door.

- Be kind now.
- Be generous now.
- Be caring now.

- Be forgiving now.
- Be prayerful now.
- Be valuable to others now.

The freedom that forgiveness offers has to be experienced. I can tell you about it, but only you can know it. It is your willingness to forgive that lifts you out of your self-made hell and brings you into the light.

Through forgiveness you demonstrate your release from your self-imposed prison. Forgiveness acknowledges your holiness, your magnitude, your oneness with God. Through forgiveness you can think clearly, and the clear memory of who and what you are returns to your mind. Forgiveness liberates your soul. Through forgiveness you find peace.

Stop and feel the simple power in the above statements of truth.

I think of the legions I have known who have made such misery for themselves because they simply cannot or will not get over and beyond a hurt from the past. The event is kept ever alive in their minds and psyches, and through constantly reliving it they continue to keep themselves in hell.

If people could only realize the power they possess, the power of their thoughts! Again, as Emerson said, we become what we think about all day long. And if we are clinging to a grievance with anger, for instance, then what we become is more angry, and that keeps us miserable.

To live in an illusion of negativity about our life is not to live in the truth of our being. The truth is that you are a spiritual being, living in a spiritual world and governed by spiritual laws.

All you need to realize is that the choice is always yours. You do have free will. You choose to turn toward the light, the spirit, or you choose to turn toward the confusion of the ego.

The ego will always instruct you that it is right to hold on to grievances, that forgiveness is folly. It is the ego that insists that what another individual or group did is unforgivable. Adhering to your ego's belief not only keeps the ego alive, it robs you of experiencing peace of mind and the shift in perception that forgiveness will bring.

If you but knew the glorious goal that lies beyond forgiveness, you would not keep hold on any thought, however light the touch of evil on it may appear to be.

—*A Course in Miracles*

Forgiveness removes you from the evil dream of what has been done to you, and this act alone releases you, offering you freedom, liberation, healing.

When we hold fast to a grievance about another, we will always see ourselves and the other as separate. Separation is a perception, not a reality. Perception keeps us engaged in a constant process of evaluation—good/bad, more/less, desirable/undesirable—an ongoing round of accepting and rejecting. Everything is always changing. Perceptions are never true because they are always based on false evidence.

Think of perceptions as a cosmic game of smoke and mirrors. All may look a certain way, but is it really? At best perceptions give us the tiniest glimpse of what may be happening. Beyond perceptions, however, lies knowledge. But we may achieve knowledge only when we have released all our perceptions. This is no easy task.

Knowledge is permanent. It never changes. It does not have degrees as perception does. Our perceptions disappear in the light as knowledge dawns in our minds, and our perceptions return to their original unsullied state of holiness.

At times our perceptions can hold some truth, but more often than not they offer us a very mixed bag—perhaps a mixed bag with a sprinkling of the eternal, but most often simply a confused mixed bag of misperceptions.

When we enter into the state of mind where knowledge abides, we experience liberation. We are no longer bound to the false "facts" or false images our perceptions give us.

Knowledge will dawn in your consciousness only when you have become aware of the illusions that have been governing you. Our minds cannot be host to illusions and the truth simultaneously. When we live mostly asleep, spiritually, we confuse the two and are unable to clearly distinguish one from the other. We can only know oneness (knowledge) or dwell ignorantly in illusions.

When we recognize our oneness with God, we then know we dwell in the mind of God.

FORGIVENESS IN ACTION:
ACTIVE FORGIVING

In your journal, make a list of everyone you feel needs your forgiveness. You can include your parents, your siblings, your grade school teachers, your cousins, aunts, and uncles, your ministers, bosses, classmates, friends, co-workers, colleagues, politicians, even yourself, and even God—whomever you feel you have a "charge" with.

Then, next to each name, write down the thing that that person needs to be forgiven for. For instance, you might write "treating me cruelly," "not seeing who I really am," or "betraying me." If you wrote yourself on that list, write down what you feel you need to forgive about yourself.

Next, while breathing deeply, look at each name on the list and silently (or aloud, if you can) say, "I love you and I forgive you." Do that for each name on the list. You may want to do it several times.

When we actively choose to be forgiving, we begin to shift our energy. If not forgiving creates negative feelings within us, choosing to forgive will create positive feelings. By stating our forgiving intention toward each person on the list, we are beginning the process of positivity in our own lives.

How do you feel your life would change if you did this one simple exercise every day for a month? Would you feel lighter, less at the mercy of your emotions, more in control of choosing what you want? Would you feel more compassionate, more loving, more generous?

Try this positive forgiving practice for thirty days, and see for yourself what shifts in your life!

CHAPTER 4

God as Source

To understand everything is to forgive everything.

—THE BUDDHA

Seldom do ordinary people make the connection between their religious or spiritual beliefs and how to bring all that into the moment-by-moment function of their lives. They fail to make the connection between what they hold as spiritual values and

- their workday;
- their hopes for the future;
- their present aspirations;
- their present and future goals;
- their relationships with family, friends, and co-workers;
- their day-to-day conversations.

The majority compartmentalize their lives into separate boxes—God and spirituality, family, home, possessions, responsibilities, career, goals, recreation, travel, education, future happiness—each in its own box. In this attempt to separate one aspect of life from another we can become isolated and confused, never quite satisfied, never quite catching the brass ring.

We may attempt to compartmentalize our lives, but we are not compartmentalized beings at our center—we are one. Therefore, our relationship with God has everything to do with our family, home, possessions, responsibilities, career, and goals.

God and spirituality are not to be tucked away to be pulled out on Sunday or Saturday or when we sit on our meditation cushion and then return it to its niche. Our spiritual awareness, the degree to which we are awake, has everything to do with every individual item in our lives. The separateness begins to melt away once we begin to realize this.

A vitally important spiritual law, the cornerstone of an awakened consciousness, is to know God as the source of all your good, all your blessings, all your abundance, all your health, all your happiness.

The source of the awesome power of Niagara Falls comes from Lake Erie, which flows into the Niagara River, which in turn directly feeds the falls. The amount of power (God) remains consistent for each one of us.

The amount of access is different for each of us, because it is determined by our own consciousness. This is fabulous news! Why? Because God as Source is vast and limitless, beyond the greatest expanse of power we can imagine. With God, everything we can ever hope for, dream, or imagine is already established.

What we must do is tap into that God energy through our own consciousness, bringing the infinite into human (physical) expression and attaining what we believe we deserve.

There are those whose accomplishments and abundance seem as impressive as the mighty Niagara Falls, and those whose lives seem to be guided by a small rivulet trickling along through a drought.

There is a simple three-part sequence that always governs our lives: (1) God as Source enters (2) your consciousness, which then results in (3) your present manifestation of good.

We're talking quantum physics here, which is all about the physical merging with the metaphysical. This tells us how everything works or doesn't work. All actions to be successful and beneficial must take place first at part 2, or altering part 3 will be only a temporary fix at best.

Attempting to alter part 1 is foolishness. To fuss with God as Source is like trying to stop Niagara Falls by your command. No matter how forceful and demanding you are, it will still follow a greater master. We don't attempt to alter God with our pleadings and promises. God is not a wish fulfiller. God is endless love and energy constantly pouring its essence upon you.

You need do nothing, for God is forever lavishing blessings upon you. The question is, Can you—your individual consciousness—welcome them in? Do you hear the guidance coming your way and respond to it?

As our consciousness awakens, we can then be aware enough to ask for help. We ask God as our Source to help us where we have difficulties in forgiving. When you feel you cannot forgive, turn within and ask your Source to make a way in your consciousness where you previously were blocked or shut down. Ask your Source to soften your heart, to open your mind.

In the future, changes will be necessary at part 3, but it is never a starting place if you are to meet with lasting, permanent success and peace of mind. This is a life process that must be followed if the desired results are to occur.

It is a divine process that each of us must awaken to if we are fully to know God as Source and not rely on our own strength. For most of us this takes much practice and faithful diligence. We are so used to carrying the weight of our lives on our own shoulders—like some modern-day Atlas—it's no wonder we are so often exhausted. By not relying on God this exhaustion is much more than physical; it is wearing us down on a mental and soul level.

To rely on God we must trust God. In order to trust God we must know God. In order to know God we must have a relationship with God. This is not some far-off God, not an angry and vengeful God of our ancestors. This is a God who is loving, caring, all-knowing, all-powerful, ever-present, closer to you than the air you breathe.

To know God as the spirit of life and love that dwells in us means we can relax. We are already nurtured, and we can always trust this divine spirit that resides within us. This God always knows what is for our utmost good. This God is always opening doors of opportunity for us. This God sets in motion cosmic events of such a magnitude that it will often take us years to comprehend their full effect.

All this and infinitely more is available to us when we perceive God as our Source. Having free will we are totally capable of saying, "No, thanks, I'd rather do it myself." Then we muddle through and become a self-made man or woman, age too quickly, and live in a state of exhaustion. We can meet with some lesser degrees of success, but such an existence can never result in the sheer joy that fills one's being when we live as cocreators with the divine.

I have known many people of financial means who are so happy that they can hardly contain their bliss. They are the spiritual cocreators.

I have known many people of financial means who

are always struggling, never really happy, and constantly on edge. These are the do-it-yourselfers who keep God behind a closed door. Their energy is locked up. Their faces do not glow with delight. They fret and worry, have ulcers and heart problems, are afraid of change, and fight for the status quo. They have only a perfunctory concern for anyone else, particularly those of lesser means or social status. They find only occasional pleasure in life and almost never realize joy. These folks are asleep, asleep to the real possibility of what could be available to them if they chose to be cocreators with God.

When we are asleep to God as our Source, we do not have the consciousness that is attuned to our good—receptive to a divine idea. We do not hear God's voice softly directing us, because our ears are too filled with the grating sounds of the world. We do not think forgiveness is necessary. The idea has never occurred to us.

When we copartner with God as our Source, we seldom will go off to dwell in a cave. To paraphrase Jesus Christ, we will live in the world and no longer be a part of it. We then govern our world and are no longer governed by it.

This does not mean that we begin to live in a bliss that is totally out of touch with physical reality. It does not guarantee that we will never have setbacks, missed opportunities, or challenges in life. But it does mean that we know how to get back up, brush ourselves off, and begin again. We always know beyond doubt that God is with us.

In the recent past I felt guided to apply for a unique position at a spiritual institution. Even though I was blissfully happy having brought three decades of pulpit ministry to completion and having no intention of entering the spiritual workforce again, the spirit tapped at my heart and I applied for the position.

Quickly I became one of the finalists for the position, having had a very positive first interview. I had the feeling it was mine if I decided in the end that I wanted it.

What happened then was most startling to me. I was not invited in for the final interview. Everything had been going swimmingly. I was stunned. I was well aware of my skill set and qualifications and renewed desire to serve.

Having told only my closest intimates of my intention to once again dive into the deep end (I knew they would question my sanity), I now had a handful of people to call and inform that for whatever reason I was no longer in the running.

To a person each one was first relieved, since each one had been concerned that I not be hurt. Hurt is not a place I would go at this juncture of my spiritual journey. Hurt comes from a wounded ego, and my soul—after years and years of spiritual work—is quite healed. But I was stunned by the organization's decision.

A close colleague who was on the inside of this organization was livid. He kept saying he was so concerned I was hurt, and I assured him I didn't go there anymore. I told him I was stunned, and beyond that I was confused. How, when my internal guidance had been so clear, could I have been so mistaken?

I prayed about this aspect unceasingly for about a week, and in a time of quiet contemplation an image of the Old Testament story of Abraham and Isaac came to mind. In the story the patriarch Abraham is told to build an altar where he is to sacrifice his cherished son, Isaac. The Hebrew God is not a god into human sacrifice, so something else is going on. But what?

As a metaphysical minister I always search for the deeper, inner meaning behind the appearances of a story. Abraham means "father of a multitude." He represents the first steps of faith—to be obedient to the spirit and its guidance. Isaac means "divine sonship, joy, laughter."

The tale of Abraham's near sacrifice of his son illustrates that we must be willing to give up that which we treasure most in order to have the deepest relationship possible with God. When we become willing to give up everything we have held dear, then we are shown we do not need to sacrifice anything.

Personally I was willing, because I felt called, to give up my totally serene new life if that was what God would have me do. Because I was willing, I did not then need to do it. Therefore that other door closed, and I could continue to live without stress and demands, living in a tropical paradise.

Although I was truly confused at first, that is no longer the case, and I now see the whole episode as one where I showed my willingness to the spirit of God within me, who I can imagine saying, "Okay, just checking to see if you are still on course. Forget about the other thing since I have greater work for you to do, with far less stress." I practiced forgiveness of self for a few days just in case I had misinterpreted my inner guidance. I always want to stay clear and on course.

What we do, what we think, what we have are never permanent conditions, even though we think they are. The Buddhists stress the impermanence of life, although it is difficult for most of us to realize or fully understand it. And if we seem to be in the dark, what we must remember is that God is Source, always.

A Reason, a Season, a Lifetime

"A reason, a season, a lifetime" was a throwaway comment a colleague once made as he and I discussed relationships during a heartfelt luncheon conversation. Those simple words ignited in me a flood of memories as well as many feelings on my past and current relationships.

The very next Sunday a stylish middle-aged woman

asked me, "May I come and see you? This week my best friend of thirty years just 'divorced' me and won't discuss it with me. After thirty years she won't even have a conversation." The woman was wounded. Her soul had been pierced by one she had considered her female soul mate for a lifetime. But in her friend's mind it was over.

An enduring relationship that had long nurtured and sustained the two of them through joyous times—weddings, births, social events—and challenging times—illnesses, deaths, divorces—was no more. They had raised their children together, but it was done. The sense of loss for this woman was enormous. The internal questioning and the emptiness was much like the aftermath of the unexplained death of a loved one. At her age, fifty-six, she could never repeat such a friendship. What she had for decades believed to be a relationship for a lifetime was revealed to be a relationship for a reason. And the reason was complete and currently without understanding.

There are those we presume will be in our lives for a lifetime—our parents, our siblings, our spouse, our children, our best friends, other close family members, our business partners. Then the vagaries of life occur, and the son pulls away from the family and refuses further communication. This causes suffering for everyone in the family. Without apparent reason the middle-aged husband walks out of his marriage by announcing one morning at the breakfast table that he has been unhappy for years and is leaving. He says there is no hope for reconciliation. In fact, he has already secretly packed and never returns after his cereal and coffee. His wife, his children, his stepchildren are all in shock, and they suffer.

These events are real. They happen every day, and they inevitably cause much suffering. Our minds and souls count on these intimate relationships lasting forever. They are our anchors, and they can be our plumb bobs to keep us centered. But our histories and life experiences speak of something very different. True friends and family members invest tremendous amounts of self in relationships. We expect them to last forever, and then by another's choice or another's death they are no more. At such times the more we cling, the more we rehash every occurrence, every word spoken, looking for signs and meanings, the more we cause ourselves to suffer, and often greatly.

We can begin to transform the pain and shock, as well as heal our shattered feelings, when slowly we begin to realize that the relationship, in spite of its longevity and complexity, was for a reason and not a lifetime. Perhaps we do not yet understand all of the whys, but we do realize it is complete. We must in order to move on from loss and misery.

With that realization we have tremendous opportunity to grow spiritually by faithfully and regularly releasing the hurt and expectations of the past. We do this by beginning the process of forgiving the other person for pulling away, for his unskilled behavior or his refusal to communicate. It is also necessary to forgive ourselves in connection with the dismantling of that relationship. We forgive for any codependency, for not picking up the clues of the other pulling away or becoming preoccupied or disinterested.

Next it is very helpful to feel grateful for the good that was in the relationship—the happiness, the joys, the sharing of significant times, the life lessons. Doing so will keep your heart energy open and soft. To go through such a loss does cause much pain, but no one needs to come out of it with a hardened heart that will either compound or bury the hurt.

Keep forgiving, keep blessing and letting go until you literally feel the shift inside you. An affirmation many have used successfully is: "I forgive you, I bless you, I release you, I let you go." Repeat this affirmation for the days, weeks, or months necessary until a positive shift happens within you. When that occurs add to the end of the affirmation, "I love you." This new spiritually aware understanding brings about a shift in your consciousness, and you will begin to experience the miracle of healing.

REASON. Some relationships come into being for a specific purpose. When that purpose is fulfilled, there is an amicable parting and no further contact is needed. Life goes on for all parties. Examples of relationships with "reason" include patient-physician, client-attorney, student-teacher, buyer-salesperson. When the purpose for the relationship is fulfilled, good-byes are said, and that is that.

SEASON. Some relationships naturally last for a specified length of time, a "season." Examples include a soldier with his commanding officer and comrades during a tour of duty, a child with a counselor during summer camp, a student with a host family during an overseas exchange. The relationships end, as expected, and hopefully everyone involved has grown because of them.

LIFETIME. These are obviously the most important relationships. Children and parents, a united couple, friends, loving siblings—by their very nature they are designed to last a "lifetime."

What throws us off our underpinnings is when the relationships we believe will last a lifetime, as long as we have a breath to breathe, are yanked away from us. I asked Sharon, the woman whose best friend "divorced" her, if she still thought of her former friend. "Oh my," she responded, "I think of her every single day. She may be out of my life, but she'll never be out of my heart."

The poignancy and wisdom of "a reason, a season, a

lifetime" could not be more dramatically illustrated than where I sit as I squeeze in some time writing. I am trying to get comfortable on a hard wooden bench at the Cuyahoga County Courthouse, having come to lend support to a close friend at her first hearing in what promises to be a long ordeal of divorce. She thought the love of her life would last forever. It lasted nine and a half years (thirty-eight seasons).

Sitting here in this seemingly endless marble corridor of sorrow, I can see so much suffering and sadness in the faces of those all around me lining the benches. Where once there had been love and hope, expectancy and dreams, there is now bewilderment, anger, tears, and unmet aspirations. The "lifetime" has turned into emptiness. Hopefully with time and reflection and forgiveness a new and brighter day will emerge.

We can begin to transform our shattered feelings by slowly coming to the realization that our relationship, despite its length and involvement, was for a reason and not a lifetime. We probably don't yet know why it ended, but we are aware that it is definitely over. We must continue to let it go and forgive, and to be grateful for what it was and for how long it lasted. This understanding brings about a shift in consciousness. When that happens, our hearts open once again and the miracle of healing must occur.

I have seen individuals who are grounded in the truth

of their being come through the most difficult challenges imaginable and emerge stronger than before with even greater resolve. I, too, have lived this, many times.

In my book *A Course in Love*, I wrote about soul-mated couples who lived in holy unions. One such couple was Felicia—a longtime devoted member of my staff—and her husband, Luis. A young couple very much in love, they were the parents of three girls, the youngest being a child with spina bifida who struggled with many physical difficulties in her early years.

Felicia and Luis stood together and, with the best physicians available, met all the youngest daughter's physical challenges. Their abiding relationship remained unshaken. They felt that nothing worse could occur. Then, the unthinkable happened.

Luis, a solid physical specimen of a young man who had once played for the Cleveland Indians' Triple-A team, became sick. He began to lose weight. He saw doctor after doctor. One told him the weight loss was nothing to worry about. But he and Felicia were worried when, in one month without dieting, he lost thirty pounds and much of his muscularity. No physician had an answer, and the only diagnosis forthcoming was acid reflux disease.

As I watched his health deteriorate, I had a sinking feeling in my soul that I could not push away. My husband, David, who also knew that something of a very serious nature was wrong, finally had a heart-to-heart talk with Felicia. "Listen to me," he said forcefully to her. "Luis does not have acid reflux, and you've got to find a doctor who can uncover what it is."

That very week Luis saw a doctor who is a mutual friend to us all, a very conscientious and caring practitioner who immediately set up appointments with a top specialist. It took over a month to uncover the rapidly growing cancer, a difficult-to-diagnose type that had invaded Luis's endocrine system. A grim diagnosis followed.

Luis's and Felicia's faith was strong. He was young, only thirty-five, and had been so very strong, an Adonis type. He would overcome this. He pursued traditional and nontraditional therapies . . . to no avail. Although Luis remained fully connected to his spirituality and felt he could overcome the cancer, his body could not. From that first month of weight loss to his final night, Luis lasted thirteen months. (I am reminded of what the Dalai Lama wrote: "Some people who are sweet and attractive, strong and healthy, happen to die young. They are masters in disguise teaching us about impermanence.")

For Felicia the loss of her soul mate was unspeakable and unimaginable. She was numb and the mother of three young daughters who no longer had their doting daddy. It was a year and a half after his death before Felicia could just barely begin to allow the sun to once again shine on her face. She never for a moment neglected her grieving youngsters, reaching beyond her grief to give them all the love she had, and her daughters have had grace upon grace showered upon them.

Felicia has always been grounded in her spiritual path. Not even the terrible illness and death of her beloved husband has shaken the truth she knows. Knowing God as her Source meant that, even without Luis as the breadwinner, she and her daughters would always be provided for.

In fact, Felicia still receives 80 percent of her husband's salary. A baseball foundation headed by longtime Major League catcher Joe Garagiola paid their mortgage for several months and all of Luis's funeral expenses. The Cleveland Indians set up a local trust fund.

A close friend of Luis's who owns a sports bar and restaurant held several fund-raisers and sold T-shirts with a quote from Luis from his last public appearance, at the ceremony where he was inducted into the Cleveland State University Athletics Hall of Fame. At that banquet an almost unrecognizable Luis stood before a hushed room and in a barely audible voice expressed his gratitude for his education and being able to play baseball. Then, with piercing eyes and in a voice barely above a whisper, he said, "Have something to fall back on, like your education, because you never know when you'll be taken out of the game."

In a room filled with former athletes also being inducted into the Hall of Fame, who were there with their families and friends, everyone was in tears. Luis received a standing ovation, and a month later he was taken out of the game.

Felicia and her daughters have continued to heal over the years. Witness to her abiding faith can be seen at work constantly in her life. Although life is changed forever when a loved one dies, it can still be filled with grace and blessings. Most of us will never go through the agonizing death of a young spouse, but it is vitally important for all of us to fall back and into the arms of God.

Very painful and challenging events can happen in life that cause us to suffer deeply. When we are disconnected from the spirit, our suffering and pain seem meaningless. Life itself seems meaningless. But when we know our oneness with the One, although we still have times when we suffer, life itself has meaning for us as we remain grounded in our relationship with God.

God is the source of our life, health, joy, fulfillment, love, happiness, peace, abundance, forgiveness. God is our source for everything.

To help establish this consciousness, choose any or all of the following affirmations, or create your own.

God is my Source.
God's power is infinite in my life.

God is my Source.
God's avenues of expression for me are limitless.
God is my Source.
God sees me through this difficulty.
God is my Source.
God teaches me forgiveness.
God is my Source.

This is the first step in changing a long-held idea or attitude. Initially our minds can present many challenges to us when we introduce a new idea or begin to alter an old, dearly held belief—no matter how false it may be.

In Buddhist teachings working with the mind is called "training the puppy." I love that. It is so descriptive of our immature, ornery, playful minds that drift all over the place and need constant attention and training.

A practitioner at my former church says to the wandering mind when it is off and running on some tangent, "Stay. Stay. Stayyy. Stayyy."

Can you see your mind as an untrained puppy? Our minds are full of potential, power, and enthusiasm, but until trained it can wreak havoc in your life. There are many ways to engage in mind training. An effective one is through the use of affirmations, as well as telling the mind to stop when it starts obsessing. "Stayyy" when it wanders off into lack thinking or any form of negativity.

FORGIVENESS IN ACTION:
CLEAR-MIND MEDITATION

An essential, effective way to train the mind is through meditation. There are many versions of meditation, or "being in the silence." But one essential technique to bring your mind under control is to clear your mind of all thought during meditation. This is not easy, but it is worth your commitment to it. First of all, you need to meditate daily and not use any excuses to skip this time. Start with five to ten minutes of being alone in a quiet place where you won't be disturbed. Gradually increase your time to thirty minutes or more.

When you begin to achieve a state of deep meditation with no thought interfering, both mind and body relax and are refreshed. And as your mind becomes more and more clear, your forgiveness techniques become more and more easy and meaningful. A clear mind is connected to God, and you begin to deeply understand how forgiveness leads you to oneness with your Source.

Once the idea of God as Source has been introduced, and until it is fully established, it needs to be affirmed, contemplated, and explored until we know in our hearts and souls that it is true. As the Buddha said, "Believe nothing, no matter where you read it, or who said it, no matter if I have said it, unless it agrees with your own reason and your common sense."

CHAPTER 5

Forgiveness Leads to the Good Life

*To forgive is to set a prisoner free and
discover that the prisoner was you.*

—LEWIS B. SMEDES

If you have been pursuing your spiritual forgiveness work, you should by now be noticing some shifts in consciousness. You may have noticed life becoming even more intense or experiencing greater upheavals than you are used to. Do not fear. Do not give up. What is occurring can be spiritually explained using an old metaphysical term: chemicalization.

There are many excellent New Thought metaphysical teachers today, but some of those from the distant past were among the very best—Charles Fillmore, Myrtle Fillmore, Wallace Wattles, Ernest Holmes, Dr. H. Emilie

Cady, to name a few. Dr. Cady was a great one to teach her students of a hundred years ago about chemicalization— the physical reaction that takes place in an individual who is studying and applying new spiritual truths to replace his or her old, fixed belief systems.

There literally takes place within the person a chemical reaction or response. For example, gastrointestinal or respiratory problems may mysteriously arise. The person may become prone to colds, flu, or rashes.

A friend of mine experienced chemicalization when she was beset with one apparent viral assault after another. She was hospitalized twice in ten days, and nothing that was prescribed improved her condition. She was feeling sick, lethargic, frustrated, and confused.

What was going on was that her ninety-six-year-old mother, who had always been independent, vital, and active and was still working as a registered nurse, was diagnosed with Alzheimer's disease. Her daughter took the diagnosis far more negatively than did her mother. Like many children of long-lived parents, she never considered her mother's mortality. It was the daughter who was in the hospital shortly after her mother's diagnosis.

She is a seventy-year-old only child who never knew her father and who has never known the death of anyone close. She is sick at heart, in her gut, in her soul, and not surprisingly she is suffering mysterious viral attacks. She is experiencing a high dose of chemicalization. Her old beliefs have met the current facts. An old belief meeting current facts equals internal havoc.

A recognized problem can always be more easily resolved than an unrecognized one. When this daughter deals directly with the physical reality of what is occurring in her mother, she can begin to heal herself. To remind ourselves of what Ralph Waldo Emerson said: We become what we think about all day long.

When appearances don't look promising, if we stay the course and deal with what is, good always arises. John Lennon is attributed with saying, "Everything will be okay in the end. If it's not okay, it's not the end."

As we continue deepening our forgiveness work, in time we will come to the point where we can say it was worth the time. It was worth the effort. The Dalai Lama says that we do all this forgiveness work not to change the other person; rather, we do all this work to change ourselves. We change what we think about. We change how we react. We change how we behave. We do the work. We work, we work, we work, and—voilà!—life shifts, life changes, and we find ourselves in a new, more peaceful, happier place.

Many years ago I saw a renowned glass artist being interviewed. She was asked the prices of her exquisitely beautiful glass orbs, which had magic happening in them. She said the prices ranged from $700 to $1,500, and this was in the 1980s.

The interviewer asked her how long it had taken her to create a particularly gorgeous paperweight that was priced at $900. She said it took forty-five minutes to an hour. The interviewer asked her, "How do you justify charging that much for something that took so little time to create?"

She replied, "Oh, that was sixty minutes plus twenty years." I never forgot her answer. The woman had done her artistic work for decades, and then magic or perhaps miracles happened. And now she could make a prosperous living. I'm sure she would have agreed it was worth all the time and effort to arrive at her end result.

Her commitment is similar to the commitment we need for the forgiveness work we do in consciousness. How long does it take to forgive until the need for forgiveness is no more? The short answer is: It takes as long as it takes. The long answer is that it will be determined by you and your earnestness. We can become like the glass artist and invest twenty or so years, or even a lifetime. For a fortunate few it can come quickly, because in consciousness they have entered the eternal stream of forgiveness.

The author Malcolm Gladwell speaks of needing to invest ten thousand hours working at a particular skill in order to become proficient at it. He tells the tale of Bill Gates as a young teen slipping out of his home in the middle of the night and walking to the nearby University of Washington so he could work on the school's mainframe computer; he'd stay there for three hours before walking home and crawling back into bed. He racked up twenty to thirty hours a week at the university's computer throughout high school. His mother recalled years later that she never understood why her son was so tired every morning and why it was so difficult to wake him up. By the time Bill Gates was in his sophomore year at Harvard, he was way past ten thousand hours.

Gladwell advances the supposition that those who attain extraordinary success do so because they have invested their ten thousand hours honing their skill, craft, talent, or brilliance. If a person such as Bill Gates has put forth this degree of dedication to achieve mastery and unparalleled success, what about you and I pursuing our forgiveness work? How many hours does it take to become a master at anything?

The Dalai Lama suggests we meditate four hours a day. So if a young monk meditates four hours daily, seven days a week, he would be meditating twenty-eight hours a week or 1,460 hours a year. After six or seven years of such focus, he would be nearing "nirvana." I had to practice forgiveness work on my ex-husband for a number of years—adding up to more than ten thousand hours.

A Wedding-Night Date

Sally, a lifelong friend of mine, asked me about the twelve-week series I was currently teaching on forgiveness. It apparently shocked and amazed her, for she exclaimed, "Twelve weeks! Whatever is there to say for twelve weeks?"

After she exhaled, she went on to say that the nuns at a nearby convent were soon leading a weekend retreat on forgiveness. She asked me if I thought she should go. I told her that, if she did plan to attend, she should make certain they were including effective forgiveness techniques and exercises that she could inject into her daily life in order to actually forgive.

Forgiveness is a visceral exercise, not an intellectual one. You cannot say, "Okay, I now know I have to forgive this nasty son of a gun. So I forgive you. Good-bye. It's over. I'm done."

You must know that the wounds and messages you've received from a given individual have taken place on a cellular level. Let's liken it to the surgery of the soul it's going to take to forgive and get rid of them. We need techniques in order to develop skills we can use in our daily lives, moment by moment if necessary. We have to learn techniques in order to become proficient pianists. We must have voice techniques to become skilled vocalists. We must learn glass-blowing expertise to become proficient glass artists.

Then I asked Sally, "Will you be working on Frank?" Frank was her first (and only) husband; they had divorced. "How much forgiveness work have you done on Frank?"

"Hmmm," she replied, "I never thought of it."

My heart sank. Then, I must admit, I yelled at my dear friend. *"You never thought of it? He had a date on your wedding night with another woman, and you never thought of it? You never thought there was a need to forgive him?"*

The story of her first marriage is still one of the worst relationship stories that I can recall. As unbelievable as it sounds, he indeed had a date on their wedding night with an old girlfriend. I said to her, "You have an ocean of forgiveness work to do with this man. Frank was unconscious, cruel, selfish, self-centered, narcissistic. He had a date on your wedding night, and you never thought of forgiving him?"

I was on a roll, and I kept talking. "Do you not realize that on a visceral level this bore inside of you and nearly mortally wounded you? Do you not realize that somewhere in your cells, muscles, skeleton, organs, heart that energy is still festering?" Then I paused.

After a moment Sally sheepishly replied, "Maybe. I just never thought of it."

A psychiatrist friend of mine says that not everyone is psychologically minded. What does this mean? It means that people do not think that what is staring them in the face has any significance or meaning or importance. It is important. It is of ultimate importance.

It is little wonder that my friend has not met a new partner, since this trauma from decades ago is blocking any future happiness. It may be ancient but it still needs to be healed. It is still living inside of her. She needs to get down deep into her psyche and do forgiveness work of grand proportions. And first, she must be willing to do that work.

The question is, How much are you willing to do to shift your consciousness? Are you willing to do your ten thousand hours of soul work? Are you willing to pray, and would you go so far as to fast, to actually go without food? Fasting from food for short periods of time can help us shift our energy around experiences, and also help keep us focused on the outcome we want. I recommend that if people want to try fasting from food intentionally (meaning, doing it with a specific intention), they begin small, perhaps for a half day, and then build to a whole day. If you do try this, please do so carefully and mindfully.

Fasting from food can make a shift, but fasting from negative beliefs is even more important. Fast from talking about your problems, from dwelling on your problems within yourself, from gossiping about anyone or anything, from misusing your imagination. If you don't, you create more misery for yourself.

When we are dealing with something huge, it may be healed only by an enormous amount of work (prayer and fasting).

The adult son of a minister friend of mine was arrested, convicted, and sent to prison. He was not involved in the actual crime, although he bore some of the penalty by simply being at the wrong place at the wrong time.

My minister friend was distraught, and once a month he would drive five hundred miles to visit his son in prison. He prayed unceasingly, and in addition to his prayer work he went on a complete food fast every Friday. He said, "I am willing to do whatever I need to do to shift the energy of this situation. I am willing to fast every Friday and pray every day until the energy shifts and my son is vindicated."

Have you ever wanted something so badly that you were willing to fast once a week for years? That was what my friend did to assist his son in getting out of prison. He did this for eight years until his son was released. He did the work necessary for forgiveness. He believed that fasting would assist in removing the negative energy and he was willing to do it. He embraced the old biblical teaching that only through fasting would the most difficult situations be resolved.

We often want forgiveness work to take a few hours or a few days. But I've found that it's more important to be thorough and thoughtful in your work, rather than just to be fast. The Buddhists, who believe in reincarnation, teach that some forgiveness work may even take eons and eons. So that you can accomplish total forgiveness in this lifetime, follow these teachings and change will come; shift will happen. Don't give up, no matter what. Keep on keeping on.

In my book *A Course in Love* I used the iceberg as an example of the unforgiveness we carry. Only 10 percent of the iceberg is above the surface of the ocean. So the 10 percent that we are aware of represents what we can work on at any one time.

So we forgive, forgive, forgive until that 10 percent is healed. Then the unforgiven parts of us rise to the conscious mind so we can heal them. In time we will be able to heal our entire "iceberg," but it takes our time, our commitment, and our endless patience.

If Sally were to write a list of what she was angry about with her ex-husband, beginning with that 10 percent that she could easily see, Sally's list might look something like this:

- He had a date on our wedding night.
- He cheated on me our whole marriage.

- He weighed me every morning because he wanted me to look perfect.
- He worked late every night with his "lesbian" secretary.
- He would come home late after being with her and demand sex.
- He has now been married to his secretary for twenty years.
- He was mean, self-centered, and always criticized me. He was so unkind.

Then, to get to the lower 90 percent of her psyche, she would first heal this 10 percent. Then more hurt and anger would rise to the surface, and she could work on that, and so on. To begin working on the 90 percent, Sally might write: "There are decent men to meet and date." This simple affirmation might cause her subconscious mind to scream: "This is a lie. This is ridiculous." But she'd need to keep saying it over and over and also writing it fifteen to twenty times a day until she could agree to it and come up with some examples of decent men. Then Sally could be on her journey of healing and heading for a breakthrough.

The Dalai Lama, quoting the Buddha, says, "I point the way, but all the work has to be done by you."

The 90 percent that needs to be forgiven and healed is

not going to be pleasant or welcoming, but it will come to the surface so you can be healed. Write your affirmations every day until you begin to come into agreement with them and are fully into the healing process.

When we are in our soul-healing process, know that those closest to us can hurt us the deepest through their betrayal—a spouse, father, mother, sibling, partner, or lifelong friend.

If it takes prayer and fasting for weeks or years, you will say it's been worth it, because you have been set free. You are no longer burdened by those phantoms from the past. It's getting better. Every day in every way it's getting better and better. And you will never say, like my dear friend, "I never thought of it." You are liberated.

Sally did that forgiveness work. She focused on it for months. It was obvious she had entered a new phase in her life when she said, "I have forgiven Frank and now all the emotional charge is gone. I have compassion for him. I have compassion for myself. I can be grateful for our two children and four adorable grandchildren. When I now see him at a family reunion, he's like someone I barely knew in high school." She paused for a moment, lost in thoughts of long ago and far away.

Sally, like others who have been willing to do the deepest forgiveness work, had a major shift in consciousness. Years later she still is not in a partnership. "I believe," she said, "God does not want me to have a life partner." I kept my mouth shut. I have finally learned to love my friends for where they are in life and to be somewhat tactful and circumspect when I don't agree with what they say.

The way I see it is that God neither wants nor doesn't want Sally to be with a man. God is not Santa Claus, nor a matchmaker. God is the life current of the universe. God is love. If Sally truly desired a committed, loving relationship, she would attract it—as long as she removed all the blocks to love's presence.

I know in every fiber of my being that God is love. God loves all of us and wants us to be happy. If being in a loving relationship is what will make you happy, you can have it. Just make sure it is what you really want and be willing to do your part in making it happen. If Sally truly desired a loving relationship, she would attract one. *That which you are seeking is seeking you.* It makes me wonder if Sally still has more of that 90 percent forgiveness work to do before she feels free enough to enter into a new relationship.

The Vine around Her Heart

Moira was like so many women in that she was very impressionable when she was young. At twenty-two she was sophisticated, knowledgeable, and worldly in so many ways, but not so in many other ways.

One night in New York City she walked into a room, instantly spotted Paul among the partygoers, and in a heartbeat knew he was going to be a most significant man in her life. It took a year before the two of them deeply connected, but during that time span, whenever she saw him her heart would flutter.

As Moira reflected on that time, she dreamily stated that it was really like it was a different life. She was drawn to his brilliance, his polish, his humor. He had a man-about-town quality, yet at the same time she felt safe whenever they were together. In those early years she felt that they were deeply connected, and she knew he was the love of her life.

Over time their relationship deepened even more, and they moved in together into a beautiful apartment that she still owns. Looking back on it later, Moira told me there were signs that all was not well in her paradise; she just wasn't particularly good at reading them.

Moira came from a family of upstanding men of integrity and noble behavior. In her naïveté it did not dawn on her that these were not the characteristics that shone through Paul. He was a high-powered attorney, gone a great deal of the time—on business, he would say. Meanwhile she was busy on her own, building a career in television production.

One day, five years into their relationship, she received word that her mother, whom she dearly loved, had suddenly died. Right after that, without warning or discussion, Paul moved out.

Moira was, as she described it, shell-shocked. Grieving for her mother and in tremendous pain from Paul's sudden departure, she attempted to reach him but ran into a brick wall. No phone call was ever returned, no letter answered.

As time passed, Moira was doing the best she could to pick up the pieces of her life when she met a business associate for lunch. Her opening greeting to Moira was, "I was surprised you were not at Paul's marriage this past weekend." It took everything she had within her to maintain her composure. Somehow she survived the lunch without becoming unraveled.

She then called his office one more time and, to her surprise, Paul answered. She said to him curtly, "We have to talk."

"Of course," he replied, "let's have breakfast." Once again she was surprised. So a date, time, and place were chosen for breakfast. He was a no-show.

That was the last straw for Moira. This time this tall, slim, well-heeled woman marched to Paul's place of business and into his office.

"Why are you here?" He sounded shocked.

"To talk about you, me, and your wife."

His secretary was standing in the room, and Moira said, "Would you ask your secretary to leave?"

"No," he responded, "she won't leave."

So Moira decided to head for the exit, and Paul caught up with her, walking beside her, holding her elbow. He exclaimed, "How could you do this to me? I always loved you."

Moira found his response very difficult to swallow. But the topper came when he told her his new wife was his secretary, the same woman Moira had always had to go through to reach him on the phone.

Moira later recalled, "I realize now that he was acting like a stupid man, but he had my heart. I had to work long and hard to get him completely out of my system. Occasionally I would run into him on the street or in a restaurant. It was quite painful. But I think, in his own odd way, he did love me."

Moira had a lot of forgiveness work to do. Her approach to forgiving Paul was similar to a Buddhist technique. Initially she approached the entire healing process through the intellect, reasoning that her sorrow and grief were only hurting her. Also, Moira reasoned, many people had gone through betrayals and survived and gone on to find happiness. Plus, there were many, many people who had gone through much worse things than she and yet had gone on, in time, to find fulfillment in their lives.

Still, her heart and soul seemed possessed by him.

Then in a meditation she saw an image of a vine wound around her heart, holding her in a tight grip. In subsequent meditations she imagined that she was literally freeing her heart from this vine, getting it out of her heart and away from her. It was a slow process, but with repetition it began to work. It felt to Moira that Paul's energy was being removed from her heart. It was a very powerful experience. It was exhausting, yet liberating. She was calm and sad simultaneously. She was healing.

A Course in Miracles calls such a remarkable event a "holy instant." I believe Moira had a holy encounter with the divine. The unrelenting pain and suffering were no longer holding her down. She could now pick up her life and move forward toward being the highly respected and successful businesswoman she became.

Today Moira looks upon Paul with compassion, because in spite of his outward success he always felt he wasn't up to the mark. "He did the best he could," she reflects, "it just wasn't good enough.

"I never think about or talk about that part of my life anymore. It was as if it was a different lifetime. As awful as it was, it turned out to be a blessing in many ways."

Moira's is a wonderful example of how, when we have thoroughly done our forgiveness work, we do forget. We never think of it anymore. The past no longer has a hold on us. It is no longer entwined around our hearts.

FORGIVENESS IN ACTION:
FORGIVENESS MEDITATION

Enter into a meditative state. See the person who has hurt you sitting across from you—just there, not interacting with you in any way. Open your heart and begin to send healing, forgiving energy from your heart to the other person. Silently or aloud begin to affirm, "I forgive you. I let you go, I set you free. All cords that connected us are dissolving now and forever more." Do this until you sense a shift in consciousness. This may take several repetitions or even longer. Do it until you feel it.

CHAPTER 6

The Karma of Forgiveness

Forgiveness says you are given another
chance to make a new beginning.

—DESMOND TUTU

My uncle Earl from Fresno, California, was a dear, kind, loving man who fathered five exceptional children. He was clearly loved by them all and by his wife, my father's sister Carmella. This was never more evident than when he moved into the last stages of his life.

Dealing with a severe illness, he was hospitalized for the last time. On his final day he was surrounded by his devoted wife and children as he drifted in and out of consciousness—mostly out.

As families often do for some distraction, they had the TV on in the background. The show *Wheel of Fortune* was on. It was the final contest, and the letters that were turned showed something that looked like: SP_ _ E

THE _ _ _   _ _ _ SP_ _ _   THE _ H _ _ _. Uncle Earl roused from an unconscious state, sat straight up in bed, and in a loud voice proclaimed: "Spare the rod and spoil the child."

The family was flabbergasted. Then he lay back down and, a short time later, died.

What I later learned was that Uncle Earl, though quite loving to his family, was very prejudiced against gays, African Americans, liberals, and just about anyone who didn't act, think, and look like him. So, while they loved him dearly and mourned his passing, they also felt like they needed to complete the circle and be honest about his limitations and prejudices, so they could heal all such judgments and negativity in their family. Did the family have forgiveness work to do? Yes. Did the family have karma together? Yes. Many of the people in Earl's family have done forgiveness work and have been set free from any limitations that Earl, as the patriarch, might have left. This allows them to love Earl and to honor him, but also learn from his limitations.

Virtually all families have forgiveness work to do and karma to share together. Otherwise we would not be families. Families are great training grounds for forgiveness and healing.

A student with an inquiring mind recently said to me, "The part about Unity's teachings I don't get is that you do not believe in sin and retribution. Where is the impetus to spiritual insight and moral behavior? What makes people do good and not live wild, reckless lives?"

I responded, "We don't believe in sin, but we do believe in karma and also believe that we are innately good."

Karma is an exacting law that takes into account all the cycles of our lives—past, present, and future. I believe that Jesus summed up karma well when he said, "What we sow so too shall we reap." And karma is not just what we have sown in this lifetime. Rather, it is what we have sown through eons of time. Each one's karma has been accumulating lifetime after lifetime.

Through life we plant seeds of behavior, seeds of consciousness. If these seeds are not watered by us through our attention, thoughts, prayers, and actions, they will remain more or less dormant.

This phenomenon takes place in nature. All uncultivated seeds land on the earth either by dropping directly below their host or by being spread far and wide by the wind or birds or other creatures. Without sufficient rain those seeds lie dormant. This state of dormancy can last for decades until the conditions of nature are just right.

My husband, David, and I have observed this firsthand on our beloved island of Molokai. Like most tropical islands, Molokai has a rainy, lush end and a dry, arid end. The west end of Molokai is very dry. And sometimes the drought on that end continues for years. In one such instance after an extended dry spell, extensive heavy rains came and turned what looked like dead weeds into miles of lush, multihued green growth. The west side of Molokai looked like an entirely different island.

Where did this lavish growth come from? It had always been there. It had just been dormant. The rains awakened the sleeping seeds to life, just as the rains of spiritual thought cause the seeds of consciousness to bloom.

The seeds of goodness, love, and forgiveness are in us just as the seeds of anger, suffering, and hatred are. And whichever seeds we are watering will come into full bloom and become our karma. We carry that karma from lifetime to lifetime.

Eknath Easwaran writes in his introduction to the Dhammapada, a classical Buddhist text:

> We live and act, and everything we do goes into what we think at the present moment, so that at death the mind is the sum of everything we have done and everything we still desire to do. That sum of forces has karma to reap, and when the right context comes—the right parents, the right society, the right epoch—the bundle of energy that is the germ of personality is born again.

I've observed that many people, through no particular acts of their own, have really good karma. And conversely I've seen that many, through no particular acts of their own, have really bad karma.

A Vacation from Suffering

I had a lengthy birthday conversation with my first secretary, also named Joan. Many, many years ago when she worked for me, we became friends. We may not speak for months, but we have what she lovingly calls "birthday rules." We each send heartfelt cards and always talk on our birthdays.

During this conversation with her and her husband, Mike, they were both catching me up on the recent events of their lives. They have good karma. Mike is from Ohio and Joan from California, and they met while Joan was still in high school. They corresponded long distance for a year and married the next summer, at ages eighteen and twenty-one. They have been with only each other.

They have one son, who, in the words of Alfred, Lord Tennyson (although he was describing a woman, it fits their son, Dana), is "divinely tall, / And most divinely fair."

Life always works out for Joan and Mike. Forty years later they still adore each other. They personify what the Buddhists call "good fortune."

Are they engaged in a spiritual practice? No. Do they

spend hours meditating daily? No. Do they practice tith-ing? No. Do they let many into their inner embrace? No.

Are they good people? Yes. Do they always try to do the right thing? Yes. Do they love and emotionally sup-port their son? Yes. Do they love their dogs? Yes.

Simply put, they have good karma, and they did not have to undertake ten thousand hours building con-sciousness. They both seemed to come into the world with a golden halo over their heads, and they found one another.

The Dalai Lama said, "Our lives are conditioned by karma. They are conditioned by endless cycles of prob-lems. One problem appears and passes, and soon another one begins."

Joan and Mike appear to have few problems. The Buddha stated with regard to karma, "What is reborn is our habits." I sense that the two of them are on a vacation from suffering. Their collective past has brought them to where they are today. They truly are the exception and by no means the norm for those clearly on a path of awakening. Although between the two of them and with their son, their life appears to be free from suffering, they both have relationship problems with siblings and aging parents. So they, too, have their opportunities to forgive.

One celebrity chef, whom I have met a couple of times, isn't, in my opinion, particularly outstanding at his chosen profession. What he does have is incredible karma. Everything he touches turns to gold, and he is very popular. He is in the midst of many other chefs who have more skill, more education, more creativity. But none of them have the amazingly good karma of this celebrity chef, who owns several restaurants, has his own TV show, and is frequently a guest on several other TV shows.

One young, classically trained chef I know said to me, "What does he have that I do not have?" I replied, "Good karma. And we both know that you have miserable karma."

A friend of mine gasped when I told her of this exchange, and she exclaimed, "You did not tell him that!" I responded that I indeed did tell him that, and I did so to help him understand his suffering.

This young man's early life circumstances were deplorable. His father, a promising young physician, died when his baby son was not yet two. As the boy grew, his mother hung like an albatross around his neck, and she still suffocates him every chance he gives her. Even with all of his skill and talent and his pleasant demeanor, his life efforts are most often strangled by the negative karma that goes before him.

What does he need to do? Everything! Everything imaginable to shift the energy that stops him from succeeding at every turn. He needs to engage in every forgiveness technique he can learn. He must practice generosity, loving-kindness, doing good works, being a blessing to everyone he encounters, writing affirmations, and practicing forgiveness.

It is not about his having more talent, skill, or luck. It's about shifting his karma so he can attract good, and only good. When he has the necessary commitment and does the necessary work, he will no longer produce painful situations and an unfulfilled life. He needs to get mighty busy in putting in his ten thousand hours.

If we make the same mistake over and over again, it becomes a habit; the ensuing, endlessly repeating cycle is called "samsara" by the Buddha. Samsara, like anger, affects the individual, and after many repetitions we have less and less control over a destructive emotion such as anger.

An anger-prone person encounters anger returning to him through other individuals. Anger may also return as heart trouble, gastrointestinal upsets of all types, skin eruptions, hives, acne—the list goes on and on. When that internal anger is not properly channeled and released, it sets up shop somewhere within the body. So we work to eliminate the unrest in our minds.

The Dhammapada says, in effect, Not in the sky, not in the mountain canyons, not in any place can one hide from their negative karma. Watering seeds of anger keeps your negative karma blossoming.

Karma versus Cause and Effect

Three things cannot be long hidden: the sun, the moon, and the truth.

—THE BUDDHA

Buddhism presents us with an expanded view of karma. The commonly held view is that karma (from an ancient Sanskrit word) describes the working of cause and effect—that for every outward effect there is an underlying cause. This is true, but karma goes much deeper. True karma takes into account all of our deeds from our present life to our past lives.

The law of cause and effect has often to do with circumstantial energy. Karma has to do with all of our history.

In a previous chapter I told Felicia's story about the tragic loss of her husband, Luis. Starting at age twelve, when spring came she would feel depressed, lost, upset. These intense feelings came each spring like clockwork. Even when she was happily married and life was going smoothly, the feelings returned year after year. It was intangible. It was in the atmosphere. It was in Felicia.

After Luis died, her feelings did come back but to a

much lesser degree. What had been going on all those years? In metaphysics we say there is neither time nor space in the spirit. Had her soul somehow projected ahead to this moment from the time she was a girl of twelve? Her soul knew. It was karma.

There is no past; there is only the now. For most of us it is a most difficult concept to grasp—at least not consciously. But if we are paying attention to life, we get small glimpses. For Felicia it was a large glimpse.

If you find an unpleasant situation difficult to forgive, consider that this may be an event that began beyond this current life and that it dips into past lifetimes. You meet a new person and are instantly attracted to him or her, like Moira was. Or you immediately feel an aversion when you meet. Either way is likely to have karmic origination.

In these situations the only thing that makes sense to me is to embrace the teaching of reincarnation. Even if you've done an ocean of forgiveness work on a situation or person, if the negativity still persists, it may hearken back to a previous existence.

A number of years ago there was on my staff a male employee who was challenging beyond measure. He was extremely difficult to work with and just to be around. The parting of our ways came when he betrayed me during the most awful of circumstances.

On the surface he appeared to be intelligent, caring,

responsible—a good person. The situation of his scheming betrayal was so appalling to me that I visited a psychiatrist to explore where I had gone so wrong in my assessment of this man.

So I told the psychiatrist that he was intelligent, caring, and responsible, and she replied, "Yes, and he may also be a sociopath." At the time I did not know much about sociopaths. She said she had dealt with a number of them through the years, and the only thing one could do was to recognize the sociopath and quickly move out of his path. She also recommended I read the book *The Sociopath Next Door* by Martha Stout.

The book opened my eyes wider, and I'm better today at being able to recognize the signs of a possible sociopath. Even so, however, I have still been blindsided. Another psychiatrist friend told me that four out of ten people are sociopaths to one degree or another. Four out of ten! Little wonder our world appears so screwed up.

I engaged everything I know to rid my soul of this man, but he just would not go away. Residue of his energy kept showing up. A spiritual friend said that this seemed like no ordinary relationship and suggested I enter a deep meditation and ask to be shown the genesis of this karmic relationship.

I agreed and set aside the time, then I went deep into meditation, asking for the answer. An outrageous image from what seemed like the sixteenth century came to me.

I was standing at the side of a ship at a pier. I was very tall and gaunt. There was little to no color in the scene. There was a prisoner in chains with two burly guards on either side dragging him to the ship. When they reached me the prisoner stood up straight, glared at me, and said, "If it takes forever I will settle the score with you! I will get even with you! I will destroy you if it takes forever!" *If it takes forever!* It was as if ice water were flowing through my veins.

That memory, factual or not, caused a shift in my consciousness. Then, every day for weeks, I asked for grace and forgiveness to sweep through my mind and body, carrying with it all residual negative energy. It worked. The karma shifted. I quit having thoughts of him arise in my consciousness. I no longer encountered him. No one mentions his name anymore. It was as if, at least for me, he evaporated. Our karma together was complete.

Be willing to go all the way, to do all it takes, so that you may be healed. You always need to forgive, but there are times when you need to go beyond forgiveness and look at your karma head-on and how it interfaces with the situation.

Whether or not you call it karma, Sylvia's story is one in which a momentous amount of forgiveness was called for.

I had been visiting Sylvia's boutique over the past couple of years. Sylvia herself had chosen every unique garment and accessory in her beautiful space. Although each item was given special attention, they were priced within reason. I treasured the special pieces with which I had been gifted or that I had purchased myself.

One aspect to love about Sylvia's boutique was the personal service. When you walked into her shop you were often offered a glass of champagne or wine, a homemade cookie, or a cappuccino. It was such a warm and inviting place that it became my go-to destination for a special garment, whether for Tuesday at the office or for New Year's Eve.

One winter afternoon I was in the fitting room trying on several lovely items. As women sometimes do, I took my black knee-high tights and scrunched them down around my ankles to get a better view of my "fashion statement." I burst out giggling, for to me I looked like one of my grandmothers from the 1950s with her heavy hose puddled at her ankles and wearing a pair of old slippers. I just thought I looked so silly.

Noticing Sylvia's reflection in the mirror I said, "Don't I look like one of our grandmas?"

In a very somber voice she replied, "I never knew my grandmothers."

Even now that remembered statement gives me chills. I turned and faced her full-on. I knew she was about to tell me something awful, and she did. "My grandmothers were taken from Czechoslovakia to Auschwitz, where they were exterminated along with a number of our relatives."

She continued, "My mother and her sister survived and came to Cleveland with the eight other members of my family who lived through those horrendous years. My mother and aunt have spent many years in psychiatric hospitals."

"Oh, Sylvia," I responded softly with as much compassion as I could muster, sensing the almost indescribable agony of horror she was about to relate.

"They both physically survived the heartbreaking horror, but what they endured was enough to make one mad. It left them both without their senses. The oppression of their spirits was more than nearly anyone could endure, and as a result they were deeply and permanently damaged. This is the part of the Holocaust that I still have to live with every day."

"Sylvia," I said, "you seem so content and caring and functional. How have you gotten here?"

"Through always attempting to grasp a larger picture of reality," she answered with certainty. "Knowing that if I dwelled on the heartbreaking horror secondhand, I would be a victim of my mother's and aunt's fears. They would become mine, overtaking me, one generation later. Because I was born here, I knew I could have a good life, but I had to forgive what happened to fifty of my relatives. Only ten eventually made it out to America. If I did not want to repeat my family history, then I had to learn to forgive for both myself and them."

Sylvia really got me into thinking about what would be the end result if we were willing to do forgiveness work not just on the unpleasant things from our own past, but also for what we know about from our ancestors.

In my own family it has always troubled me that my paternal grandfather was murdered, shot in the back when he was only twenty-seven. My dad, his only child, was just under two years old. It was a horrendous trauma that changed my grandmother's life. Within two years she was forced into an arranged marriage, eventually having six more children, five of whom survived.

That heartbreaking event was significant in forming my dad's and his mother's life. Her brothers immediately stepped into the role of father for my dad, and he was deeply loved. But there was a place in his psyche that carried the hole from that gunshot through his entire life.

What if I could use spiritual practices to remove that hole? Now?

I do not know why this idea didn't occur to me decades ago, and I had never heard a spiritual teacher propose it. I'm glad it finally did come to me. The idea arose from a deep meditation, and I felt real excitement as I began to use it and experience the spiritual ramifications.

What it does is begin to heal the lives of descendants who may not even know that events in their ancestors' lives have had a deleterious effect on them, who think that the only bad moment is the present moment, the now. We bring all of our unhealed past—even parts we are unaware of—into each moment we live.

In my twice-daily forgiveness meditations I now incorporate reaching back in time and forgiving the man who murdered my grandfather. In the next chapter I explain the technique of *ho'oponopono*.

> *I'm sorry.*
> *Please forgive me.*
> *I love you.*
> *Thank you.*

There are Hawaiian practitioners of ho'oponopono who would bet their souls on the effectiveness of this ancient spiritual practice. Can you imagine survivors doing this to begin to heal the trauma that the millions of families experienced at the hands of the Nazis?

I believe we can actually right the wrongs of the past. I believe we can actually alter the course of human destiny. I view this as a major breakthrough for me on my forty-year quest for better and better forgiveness techniques.

I send blessings not only to the man who pulled the trigger and shot my grandfather in the back, but also to his parents, wife, children, and the generations of his family who have followed.

FORGIVENESS IN ACTION:
HEALING ANCESTRAL TRAUMA

Shifting ancient energy is empowering and a big deal. Find out about as much of your family's history as you can. Pick an ancestor and a situation involving an ancestor, as far back in time as possible, and begin to send a blessing.

You could start with ho'oponopono, and then you could say something like:

> *I, [your first name], now embrace your divine nature. Any and all unskilled behavior from your past is now dissolved in the light of truth, now and forever more. All energetic patterns are now dissolved. All issues have been resolved.*

Make whatever you say comfortable for your manner of speaking. Then, when you feel a connection and that this phase is complete, move one generation closer and do the same. Continue on your ancestor path until you end with yourself and self-forgiveness. The ultimate result will be your own happiness and peace of mind.

CHAPTER 7

I'm Sorry

*Compassion and loving-kindness are the
hallmarks of achievement and happiness.*

—THE BUDDHA

One of the more amazing events in my life happened not too long ago. My husband and I, who go to the same hairstylist, walked into the hair salon. We both had an appointment with this stylist, one after the other. The stylist, who is also the owner, greeted me with grave concern.

He began by saying, "I always go over my scheduling book over the weekend, but this weekend my son had a medical emergency and was in the hospital for three days. So I didn't do it."

I had no idea why he was telling me this. Then he continued, "Just now I became aware that your ex-husband's wife has an appointment with me, sandwiched between the two of you. I tried to reach her to reschedule, but she'd already left home."

Puzzled, I asked, "Why would you do that?"

"So no one would be embarrassed," he responded.

"I don't know her, and she doesn't know me," I said. "Thanks for your concern, but please don't give it another thought." I knew that I would have no trouble dealing with this woman seeing the same hairstylist, strange as that may seem.

Of course my curiosity was then aroused, and I examined every woman who came through the door. Was that pretty woman her? Was that sixty-something woman her? My ego wanted to know.

Then it was time to get my shampoo, so I sat down in the middle of three chairs in front of the hair-washing sinks. At the same time, a woman sat down to my right and reclined. I whispered to the young assistant, who had overheard my previous conversation, "Is that her?" With her eyes and a nod of her head she let me know that yes, indeed it was my former husband's wife, Patty, the woman he had had an affair with while we were in the death throes of our marriage.

I thought to myself, Isn't that just hysterical. Here we are, two long-legged women of about the same height, getting shampooed, and she doesn't know who I am.

I had left my husband more than thirty years before,

and she had been married to him for about thirty years. But I didn't care about the math. When I was married to him, all I wanted was to get out as quickly as possible. And if she was the means to that end, God bless her.

While she was getting her hair cut, I was busily observing her. She wore absolutely no jewelry, not even a wedding ring. Her nails were not manicured. Her shoes were not stylish. My observations and judgments went on and on. So much for this having no effect on me, I thought, more with amusement than anything else. After her haircut was finished, she got up, gathered her personal things, and was about to leave. I realized that it was silly not to say anything to her. And it was now or never. Life had put us together, so I decided to reach out.

Dripping-wet hair and all, I walked across the room and—standing right in her personal space—I said, "I understand you are Patty."

"Yes," she replied tentatively.

"I'm Joan Gattuso," I said, knowing she would recognize my name.

"Ah," she said brightly, "I've read your book *A Course in Love*. I regularly read your column in *Unity Magazine*. In fact, I think I've read everything you've written."

Surprised, I responded, "You've read what I wrote about your husband, my ex, in *A Course in Love*?"

"Oh, yes," she said.

"How are you with that?" I wondered aloud.

Not answering the question directly, what she said in a sad voice spoke volumes. "He hasn't changed."

"I heard he quit drinking. Has that helped?"

"For a time it did"—her voice quavered—"but then his daughter committed suicide and he's been drinking ever since."

Oh, my God! I thought. He has the worst karma of anyone I've ever known. He also had a son who died earlier, completely unexpectedly, and he was showing the early signs of dementia. I asked, "What about his youngest son?"

Patty replied, "He has no relationship with his father. He came to us and told us how his mother [long deceased from alcoholism] had sexually abused him for a number of years as a child. His dad, my husband, your former husband, yelled, 'I don't believe you!' Then his son yelled back, 'That's it! I'm done with you! Did you take any time to wonder why I would lie about such a thing?'"

I took a deep breath, then mindfully said, "It would be good to have only compassion for you and him. But I feel so sorry for you, for your life, for what you have to live with. I know the situation you're in. I simply feel sorry for you."

"You are the only one in the world who would know," she said sadly.

"Yes, I am the only one, but you stayed with him.

I had to flee before he killed me. I was so young and so afraid."

Patty nodded and said, "I was also young when I married him. I wanted to divorce him so many times, but hesitated. So I didn't, and now he has dementia."

"You are much stronger than I was," I told her. Then, "May I ask you a personal question?" She nodded weakly, and I asked, "Is he still so parsimonious?"

"Not really," she replied. "I control all the money."

"That certainly wasn't the case when I was married to him. We had separate accounts, and I never saw a nickel of his money. His cruelty, infidelity, and stinginess were at the top of my forgiveness list, which took me years to complete."

Again Patty nodded knowingly. "I have compassion for him, but I still work every day to forgive him."

She then said she had to leave and, having made an unexpected heart connection, she reached forward and we shared a warm hug. Then she left.

I know what miracles are. I know that if one practices spiritual principles long enough, including large doses of forgiveness, then when any adversity or bump in the road comes along, miracles will follow. If one lives long enough and works hard enough, then everything will be healed. In the Old Testament it states: "Stand still, and see the salvation of the Lord." Stand still and wait and know, and life will work out.

What Patty and I truly experienced in the hair salon was a "holy instant" (a moment filled with spirit, grace, and holiness; not an ordinary moment, but a God moment). With the two of us that day, time stopped and divine energy washed over us. The irony of the situation was not lost on me, for at that time I was in the midst of teaching a twelve-week series on forgiveness. I had already done plenty of forgiveness work around my ex-husband, but this experience, built on my earlier forgiveness work, took the experience of forgiveness to a whole new level.

When I recapped with my husband what had happened, David said, "You need space to move through forgiveness. You can't be in the throes of a trauma and drama and get into the mind-set of deep forgiveness. You need space."

A holy instant is a divinely orchestrated coming together of people and events that are not of our making. It is nothing more than the outcome of what every situation is meant to be. The holy instant is the result of your determination to see everyone in the world as your equal, to be forgiving, to be holy, to be released and set free.

It may sound grandiose, but I am determined to be holy, to live as though my life is holy, and therefore the actions that I take and the thoughts that I think align with that high ideal. That is why I got up from the salon's chair by the wash bowl to speak to the woman who earlier in my life I felt had deeply hurt me.

The staff at this salon where I've gone for decades know me well. As they watched the holy instant unfold, they could not comprehend what they were seeing. The manicurist said to me, "I couldn't have spoken to a woman who I knew my husband had had an affair with."

To which I responded, "It doesn't matter. The only thing that matters is that I left the marriage and forgave him and her."

We all experienced a miracle that day. And it would not have happened if I had not already forgiven him. I left the salon feeling elated and feeling God's presence. Forgiving offered that to me.

The Practice of Ho'oponopono

In the ancient spirituality of Hawaii, it was taught that old, painful memories could be transformed through the technique of ho'oponopono. Although the name is long, the healing technique is brief and to the point. One repeats over and over:

I'm sorry.
Please forgive me.

I love you.
Thank you.

A Hawaiian woman, Morrnah Simeona, from the mid- to the late-twentieth century, taught this version of the technique to large and small groups of people, including groups from universities, hospitals, and even the United Nations. In 1983 Honpa Hongwanji Mission of Hawaii named her a "Living Treasure." Among her students was Ihaleakala Hew Len, PhD.

After learning the technique, in 1984 Dr. Hew Len brought it to his place of work as a staff psychologist in the Hawaii State Hospital. He oversaw the high-security unit housing criminally insane male patients whose crimes included murder, rape, and all manner of assault. Violence in the facility was widespread, with attacks occurring against other patients and the staff members.

Three years later violence there had virtually disappeared. All restraints were removed from the patients who wore them, and new off-site activities were offered to them. Everything improved enough that peace replaced violence, and the need for this unit was no more. It closed.

Dr. Hew Len had not counseled with any of the patients. By himself he practiced ho'oponopono on a daily basis. This included accepting 100 percent responsibility for everything being experienced by him. Daily he repeated over and over:

I'm sorry.
Please forgive me.
I love you.
Thank you.

This simple prayer transformed long-held, painful memories in a seemingly miraculous fashion. In hoʻoponoponó it is believed that trauma is completely removed from our memory. The Buddhists call where these memories are stored "seed consciousness." In that memory bank everything is stored in your abiding state of consciousness.

What Hawaiian kahunas (priests) taught was that, in order to move beyond what is often called karma, there has to be a soul cleansing, a mind cleaning to rid ourselves of that state of consciousness that has traveled with us through lifetimes.

You may still wonder why you would begin a prayer with "I'm sorry. Please forgive me," when you were not the one who perpetrated the wrong.

In order to understand, you have to go deep into your soul's history, your karma, because you definitely have karma individually and collectively with the other person.

You can expand on hoʻoponopono, perhaps, by saying or writing:

I'm sorry I have thought so ill of you. I'm sorry
    you had to be the one to be so cruel and hurtful

in order for me to learn about forgiveness.
I'm sorry you had to take on that role. Please
forgive me for hating you. Please forgive me for
blaming you. Please forgive me for wanting you
to suffer. Please forgive me for praying for
negative karma to come to you fiercely and
swiftly.

With ho'oponopono you practice this technique until you experience an internal shift in consciousness, until the memory begins to fade. Then you are able to rid the mind of all stagnant residue and transform it into pure light. As you do this you free not only yourself but everyone.

Unforgiveness is a form of violence, a continuation of the deed. Unforgiveness always keeps the deed alive. An unwillingness to forgive is really an unwillingness to be healed, to be able to see the situation differently, to see it from a higher point of view.

Violence perpetuates attack, and what we attack we judge as guilty. Thus, we enter into an insane circle of violence, attack, guilt—an endless loop of judgment and unforgiveness. Any unforgiving thoughts are always attack thoughts.

Letting Go of Being Right

If you truly desire peace, you must relinquish being "right" and release attack—violent thoughts and actions. If you are unwilling to practice forgiveness, you keep the seeds of separation alive. You are watering those seeds rather than the seeds of loving-kindness and forgiveness. What you water through your consciousness, either positive or negative, will sprout and grow in your life and can be witnessed in your day-to-day experiences.

So many times I have witnessed individuals absolutely fixated on holding to their grievances, not realizing their unforgiving thoughts are keeping them in hell.

Alex is such a person. She absolutely and totally loathes her only sibling, an older brother. She has loathed him since she was three; she even has a photo of her dainty little self attempting to pull away from her ten-year-old brother, who was trying to hold her hand so the picture could be taken.

Fifty years later she still loathes him. He has never physically or sexually abused her. He has never sworn at her, made fun of her, mocked her, or told lies about her.

There is no reasonable or rational explanation as to why she has always hated him. She just does. Even if he were totally out of her life and she never consciously thought of him, she would still need to forgive him. Because of their elderly parents, however, he flies across the country three or four times a year to be with them, and that is just enough contact to set her off anew each time.

Hers is an irrational hatred. Since it is so ancient, I tend to think it must go back to a past life. But Alex cannot see that. Perhaps her chronic gastro problems, heart palpitations, and sinus troubles might have an emotional connection to continually fanning the flames of hatred. Said the Buddha, "Hatred does not cease by hatred but only by love. This is the eternal rule."

You may be thinking how miserable she must be. But if you met her you would never see her underbelly. She is bright and articulate, very witty, and caring to total strangers. But underneath this pleasant exterior is a raging inferno.

Through the years I've noticed that her unrest has escalated as she has gotten older. Her loathing of her brother hasn't lessened but has gotten more intense as each year passes.

Several times I have broached the subject of her need to work on forgiving her brother for whatever she perceives he has done to damage her. I might as well be talking to my sofa! She doesn't want to hear it. She doesn't want to get it. She doesn't want to change her story. As a result I've politely told her I'm done listening to it.

Alex's unwillingness to forgive is keeping her in hell, and in poor health at best. If she was willing to begin to forgive her brother for whatever negative perceptions she has about him, she could begin to release both of them from the evil dream in which she continues to live. Broad, sweeping forgiveness techniques are what are needed for her, because there is no recall of any specific instances that need forgiving—thoughts such as "I bless you. I release you. I forgive you. I let you go to God." Such affirmations need to be repeated over and over again. Think of a stone wall guarding a prison, in this case the prison of her unforgiving mind. Beyond that wall and deep inside the prison lie her innocence and the innocence of her brother. It would take a tremendous amount of prayer work and release to break down the wall and enter the depths of the prison.

To further assist her in doing this it would be helpful if, every time a negative thought of him enters her consciousness, she immediately releases it to God or the Holy Spirit or Mother Mary or whomever she trusts as a spiritual guide, then breathes deeply and creates a loving thought of her brother.

Whatever the circumstances of our past, we must forgive the perpetrators in our lives to experience a shift in consciousness to experience healing—to be happy. Desmond Tutu once said, "To forgive is not just to be altruistic, it is the best form of self-interest." And again from the wisdom of the Buddha: "How easy it is to see your brother's faults; how hard it is to face your own."

A wonderful technique from the Dalai Lama is called "giving and taking." In a deep meditation one visualizes sending to the other person positive emotions like happiness, loving-kindness, love, compassion—good thoughts of all kinds. Then, in the next meditation, one visualizes taking in the other's negative emotions—suffering, fear, cruelty—all the toxic emotions. Breathe all these in, when in a deep meditative state, and then breathe them out.

The Dalai Lama says that these techniques are very helpful to reduce pain and hatred, to cultivate forgiveness, and to experience peace and happiness.

When we withhold forgiveness, we become as culpable as the offender, except that we rarely are able to acknowledge our participation. So we remain in the mind-set: *I've been wronged. I am right. Damn the offending party.* This hostile state of mind will never lead to healing or resolution of any kind.

As you travel along your soul's journey of spiritual advancement, it is good to begin to be open to exploring exactly what your part was in allowing the negative situation to occur in the first place. Perhaps you were too passive, or you were not true to your moral conviction or you pretended that it didn't matter. In the first place you should have been paying more attention when inwardly you were furious.

The Dalai Lama teaches that to harbor a destructive emotion like hatred is of no use. He does not hate the Chinese, even after all the destruction they have wrought on his people and his country. In time he has totally forgiven the Chinese communists. If he can forgive the atrocities he and his people have had to endure, can we learn to follow his example and be set free?

Courtney, a young attorney, used to travel regularly between Washington, DC, Philadelphia, and New York. Over two years, each time she was in New York, she would stay with Marie, a girlfriend who lived there. They were two women at the top of their professional game, and they supported each other in a multitude of ways.

Courtney would stay with Marie about once a month. On one particular trip to New York Courtney conducted her business and arrived at Marie's apartment about ten p.m. She rang the doorbell. No answer. She called on her cell phone. No answer. She rang the doorbell again. Same lack of response. She could see lights on and shadows in the apartment, and she knew her friend was there.

For the next thirty minutes Courtney stood on that street corner in Harlem and called everyone she knew in the city. Finally she made connection with another friend, who invited her to come over and said she'd wait up for her.

Courtney never heard from Marie. She was one of her best friends . . . and now nothing. It took a lot of forgiveness on Courtney's part to get past the hurt, pain, rejection, and confusion.

Stuff happens in life, some of it very hurtful. Later Courtney tried again to reach Marie on the phone, but she never answered. By this time Courtney had completed forgiving Marie, so there was no residual pain, only puzzlement.

Two years passed, and one day Courtney picked up a voice mail from Marie. "I'm going to be in DC. Would you be willing to meet with me?" Courtney texted her back and said she would meet her at a particular café and gave her the time.

Courtney arrived at the café first. Shortly after, Marie came in, sat down, and—without saying a word—pulled a small sign out of her purse that read, *I'm sorry*.

That was it. Did these two women need to discuss this? No. Did Courtney need to be right? No. For both of them it was over. There was nothing to discuss.

Courtney had done so much forgiveness work that she was willing to meet with Marie one more time. She was willing to accept the apology in the sign. What had gone on with Marie did not matter to Courtney. To get to the place of "It does not matter" is completely liberating.

Courtney said something very profound to me: "Our friendship returned, even though what happened was very painful. But it would have been far more painful never to be in the relationship again."

Forgiveness offers everything I want.

—*A Course in Miracles*

Never in a million years would I have thought I would be in a salon getting shampooed next to my former husband's current wife, and that we would hug good-bye after experiencing a holy instant.

It's amazing what the Holy Spirit plans for us when we allow the Holy Spirit to do the planning.

Amazing.

FORGIVENESS IN ACTION: HO'OPONOPONO

To effectively practice ho'oponopono sit quietly and reflect on the importance of what you are about to do. Then repeat again and again:

I'm sorry.
Please forgive me.

I love you.
Thank you.

In doing this initially you may not quite feel it or get it. That doesn't really matter; just keep doing it and the shift will occur.

Set a schedule to do this daily for a week or two or until you feel the shift internally.

CHAPTER 8

Get Up and Forgive

*Inner peace can be reached only when we
practice forgiveness. Forgiveness is the letting
go of the past, and is therefore the means for
correcting our misperceptions.*

—GERALD JAMPOLSKY

O ur forgiveness work is not about changing others, it
is about changing ourselves. Forgiveness work pu-
rifies our filtering system. Our inner filters are packed
with a lot of history from the past. We have to constantly
cleanse our filter system through our forgiveness work.

When I was on the threshold of founding the ministry
where I served for nearly thirty years, I attended a weeklong training held at a beautiful monastery in Northern
California, the most exquisite training site imaginable.
This particular gathering consisted only of members of
the clergy.

The course was called "Making a Difference." The majority of our week was spent deeply exploring what would be necessary to have a successful ministry. Each of us would call out descriptive words as to what we thought would be absolutely necessary to have a ministry that worked.

An assistant wrote the words on a blackboard, and we finally had before us some ninety ideas—like commitment, a beautiful space, conscious and loving people, committed people, adequate parking, easy accessibility, willingness to serve, and so on.

Then the trainer pointed to each idea, asked whose it was, and had that person stand up and ask, "Is it possible to have a successful ministry without this idea?" If the idea was, say, "a beautiful space," the trainer would make a convincing argument, brief or lengthy, that it was possible to succeed without that feature. Then, when the minister agreed, the word would be erased.

One of the last on the blackboard was "lifelong dedication." The woman who had said it stood up. She had her idea written above "commitment." A rather shy and diminutive woman, after she stood up and spoke, she dug in her heels and stood firm, refusing to agree that her idea was not essential to success, refusing to have her idea erased.

All the rest of us, including the support staff, watched intently as the woman and the trainer volleyed their differing opinions back and forth, much like an intense tennis match.

Then from the back of the room came a booming voice: "I'll take over!" All heads turned in that direction. There stood the imposing figure of Werner Erhard, the founder of est, the famously intense self-improvement philosophy, which later became Landmark Education.

Werner immediately walked to the woman and in her face said, "So you think it's impossible to have a successful ministry without lifelong commitment?" Then, still in her face, he said, "What do you do?"

She seemed larger and more assured as she replied, "I'm a social worker."

"What did you do before?" he asked loudly.

Her voice became loud as well and she replied, "I was a nun."

Waving a finger in her face, Werner continued, "How long were you a nun?"

"Nineteen years," she answered as she looked directly at him.

"Nineteen years," he repeated. "No wonder you believe a lifelong commitment is necessary. But it's not. It's not true. We think we have to have certain elements in place to do our work, but we do not."

In my own life I thought I had to have a PhD to succeed. However, I don't have a PhD and yet I succeeded. People said you had to have degrees in theology to be a successful minister. I don't have them but I succeeded anyway.

Try to imagine how long it took to convince the former nun to erase her submission from the blackboard. It's hard to believe. It took three days. Three days!

In my opinion, Werner Erhard was an extraordinary teacher, one with no equal when it came to working with people. He showed the ninety of us what was important in ministry and what was not. This weeklong training with its sublime teaching became my foundation in starting a church.

On a personal level we say we'll be happy when we get that degree, make that move, lose twenty pounds, meet the soul mate, get that job, have a child, when the kids are grown. None of that will make you happy. Be happy now.

Forgiveness takes us to that place in consciousness where we are no longer attached to a building, a person, a status, a degree, or someone's behavior.

Back to that former nun. After she reluctantly agreed to have her blackboard idea erased, Werner asked her, "How do you feel?"

"I feel hurt," she said.

Without mincing words, Werner told her, "You are just 'hurt' waiting to show up!" What a great line!

What she needed was to work on forgiving herself,

her mother superior, all the mistaken teachings that had been drummed into her about God, and anyone, parent or otherwise, in her background who was the origin of her rigid attitude.

Learning Self-forgiveness

For many, self-forgiveness may be the most difficult of all. Our judgments against ourselves can go so deep that they cut us to the quick. When we continue to hold on to grievances against ourselves, we keep ourselves in hell.

You deserve to be forgiven just as much as anyone against whom you have held grievances. If you want to experience freedom, it is imperative that you forgive yourself. For whatever needs forgiving in yourself, remember: If you had known better, you would have done better. Sometimes in life we have to give ourselves a pass.

I have had to forgive myself for a great deal of unconscious behaviors from my past. The extreme for me was getting married when I knew I shouldn't—not once, but twice! It was necessary to forgive myself over and over and over. An affirmation I worked with endlessly was:

I, Joan, now completely forgive myself for all of my ignorant past behavior.

A softer, sweeter version was:

*I, Joan, now forgive myself for all mistakes from
the past.*

Forgiving yourself will bring peace to your soul and a
future different from your past. You now get to be happy.

*If you but knew the glorious goal that lies beyond
forgiveness, you would not keep hold on any
thought, however light the touch of evil on it may
appear to be. . . . And leading finally beyond all
dreams, into the peace of the everlasting life.*

—*A Course in Miracles*

Complete forgiveness brings the kingdom of heaven
so close you can reach out and touch it. Your happiest
dream will thus become your reality.

Forgiveness releases you from every evil dream you
have tried to project against a brother or a people or a
society. It makes your life more lovely than you can even
imagine.

Total forgiveness allows you to consciously enter into
miracle-mindedness. It transforms your vision, so that
what once you looked upon can be seen no more. Complete forgiveness shows you there is another way to look

at the world, as well as another way to look at everything that happens to you.

You may be shocked or you may argue with this, but the truth is: God does not forgive, because God has never condemned you or anyone else. This is a statement that is a complete departure from traditionally held religious thought. But we are going beyond traditionally held religious thought and endeavoring to reach the truth—beyond dogma and human beliefs. This may threaten many cherished beliefs, but it is the truth. God has not condemned you or anyone.

So many of our tightly clutched beliefs about God have not come from God. They have been given birth out of our collective human ego. The ego sees God as a presence to be feared, rather than known and loved. Thus, God has been created by humanity in humanity's most base image and likeness, which is contemptuous, judgmental, revengeful, disapproving, cruel, and egocentric. This is not God nature but human nature in its lowest form.

It is so important for you to explore your consciousness and uncover if you have harbored openly or covertly any godly fear and viewed God as a judging presence quick to call you to task. Ask yourself: In my heart do I view God as a loving presence who cares about me or a tyrant out to get me?

If you view God as anything other than loving, begin immediately to purify and heal those thoughts by forgiving yourself for accepting someone's false beliefs as true. This takes work. Meditate at least fifteen minutes a day on these ideas:

God is love.
God loves me.
God's love fills my mind, heart, and soul.
God holds nothing against me.
God will never desert me.
God is always with me.

A personal favorite of mine is:

In God I live and move and have my being. God
*   loves me forever.*

If you are praying for another, substitute "you" or the person's name for "me" and "my" on the above ideas.

As you forgive God, you are freeing yourself from the belief that he would ever crucify you. By daily reminding yourself of God's eternal love for you, you are systematically erasing any false thought that has ever caused you to fear God or to be suspicious or not trust him.

The mass of men lead lives of quiet desperation.

—HENRY DAVID THOREAU

God Loves You!

Madeline, the adult daughter of a most dynamic and powerful teacher who is a longtime spiritual sister of mine, was busy leading her secular life. She was content in her marriage as she and her husband raised their twin sons.

Growing up, Madeline wasn't particularly interested in her mother's writings or her spiritual work. The years passed uneventfully until there was a major health crisis with one of her boys. She turned in desperation to her mother for help (a rare occurrence). Gently her mother explained that, as dire as the diagnosis appeared, God was still God in the midst of her anguish. God loved Madeline's son who was ill, and God loved Madeline.

Madeline had listened, and as she drove home through the mountainous region, she affirmed aloud over and over, "God is with my son. God loves my son. God is with me. God loves me." Again and again, louder and louder, she repeated it as she drove. Then, to help relieve her own fears, she shouted over and over, "God loves me! God loves me! God loves me!"

Then a great awareness gripped Madeline. "Holy shit! God loves *me*!" She slammed on the brakes and pulled off to the side of the road and got out of the car. In that moment, looking up at the majestic mountains, she had gotten it. Her heart opened. Her life changed. Arms outstretched, she loudly affirmed again and again, "God loves me! God loves me! God loves my son! God loves my son!"

After she drove home, the minute she walked through the door she knew her son was beginning to heal. And without any doubt she knew that God loved her; God loved both of her sons, her husband, her mother; and God loved all humanity without ceasing.

If you have any doubts about your own faith, affirm over and over and over, "God loves me! God loves me! God loves *me*!"

The supreme accomplishment, the freedom that comes to our minds and our lives when we forgive, is something that has to be experienced. It has to be felt. It cannot be intellectually explained; rather, it is known in the core of our being. It is joy. It is eternal. It is the supreme accomplishment. It is complete fulfillment. It is happiness. It means living a life free from strife.

The late poet laureate and brilliantly spiritual Maya Angelou had her own soul realization that she was loved by God. As a guest on the Oprah Winfrey show *Super Soul Sunday*, Maya was asked by Oprah where she went for inspiration. I was surprised and delighted when she said she would read from a Unity book, *Lessons in Truth*, for her inspiration. As a Unity minister, I had no idea of Maya Angelou's love for Unity.

She told of how years ago she had a voice teacher, Mr.

Frederick Wilkerson, who held an artistic salon once a month in his home. His guests included opera singers, cabaret singers, nightclub singers, and recording artists, and they would gather and read from *Lessons in Truth*, a spiritual classic written by Dr. H. Emilie Cady.

Maya was asked to read from the book a selection that ended with "God loves me." She read it and then closed the book. Mr. Wilkerson said, "Read it again." Slightly annoyed, she read it again. "Again," Mr. Wilkerson repeated. She complied, although wondering why. Maya read the section seven times in all.

When she finished the seventh reading she began to cry, as the truth of those words and their enormity began to dawn on her. If they were true—and they were—she could do and be anything. Those words from *Lessons in Truth* helped shape her life. (You can read Maya's account in her book *Letter to My Daughter*, chapter 27.)

If you grasp the magnitude of this statement of truth, as Maya did, it can give you a major boost in shaping your life as well. God loves you! Stand in front of a mirror, look into your eyes—happy or sad, pensive or expectant—and affirm aloud with boldness, "God loves me!" Again and again. Do it twice daily, seven times or seventy times, until the awakening comes to you.

Be bold like Madeline or Maya until you realize on a soul level that God loves you. Know this not only in your intellect but in your soul, in your heart. Know it with each breath you take. God loves you. God loves you. God loves you.

Here's an uplifting, joyous exercise: While at the gym, or walking down a busy street, or riding on public transportation, glance at an individual and silently affirm for him or her, *God loves you*. And then on to the next person, and the next. Do it when you check in on your children or when you are entering a meeting. As you practice this, your life is becoming a prayer. Exercise and have fun with it. Who knows who you will encounter.

Once, when I was doing this exercise as I was driving quite a distance from home, I was stopped at a stop sign, and when the car that had the right-of-way crossed in front of me, I silently affirmed to the driver, *God loves you*. I was shocked when I realized that the driver was a congregant of mine, someone I had always been quite fond of. She was also a great distance from home. She didn't see me, and I never mentioned it. But the serendipity of the moment was quite uplifting for me.

> *Do not neglect to show hospitality to strangers,*
> *for thereby some have entertained angels*
> *unawares.*

—HEBREWS 13:2

The Christ spirit in you is blessing each person you encounter. You stand together in a holy moment in the presence of truth. For your brothers, your sisters, friends, children, lovers, parents know what they may not know for themselves: God loves you.

So what does this mean? For Maya and Madeline it meant that through the power of God they could do or be anything. It is coming to the full realization that not only are you loved by God, but with God you can do and be all things. With God you can forgive every hurt, no matter how trivial or enormous it may seem to you.

You are blessed by God's love, and you have free will, which means you can accept your blessings and reap their wondrous benefits, or you can live like an abandoned orphan, alone and fearful.

Accept that you are blessed. Know that you can be happy and have joy and peace, be self-assured, and be strong in all aspects of your life. Develop an understanding of the words "I can do and be all things through God who strengthens me."

Forgiving ourselves is often the most difficult work of all. The nun's nineteen years was a significant chunk of her life, as it would be in anyone's life, but forgiving would help her let go of any fixed ideas she had gained, during that period of time, that made her feel she was a failure, weak, or selfish and couldn't keep a commitment.

Wake Up!

Here is another extraordinary story of a wounded life and years of soul work that led to deep transformation. Elizabeth was an artistic child born into a toxic environment with shut-down, uncaring parents who were unaware of how to nurture her. She was gentle and sensitive, but her loveless upbringing began to stifle her creativity.

As the years passed Elizabeth shut down more and more. Finally at age eighteen she left home and struck out on her own. A few years later she discovered the power of forgiveness, and through her intensive forgiveness work she gradually began to leave this damaging chapter of her life behind.

I have always told my congregation that they may be looking at me, but I'm also looking at them. I remind them of that because of some of the surprising behavior, such as playing footsy or necking, I witness during a church service.

Even though Elizabeth had worked extensively on forgiveness, she still had work to do. This manifested itself in the number of dysfunctional relationships she was in through the years.

She showed up one Sunday with yet another selection. Harold, a handsome and debonair man, was with her, and they snuggled during the service. She fell head over heels for him, and he fell into deep lust, adding her to his harem of conquests.

You know how the story goes. Perhaps you've been there, but most certainly you have a friend or acquaintance who has been there:

Boy meets girl. Girl falls for boy. Boy plays around. Girl is crushed. Boy dumps girl and moves on to his next conquest. Girl is left to pick up the pieces of her life once again.

By all appearances Harold was not what Elizabeth needed or deserved, but she stayed in this doomed relationship because, as Sydney Harris said long ago, the holes in her head fit perfectly with the rocks in his.

We leap forward several years, to a time when Harold had moved on—literally—and was living in Europe. No one had seen or heard from him in several years. Then on a particular Sunday morning, when church was being held in an auditorium that seated 960 and we generally attracted one hundred or so, in walked Harold, and he sat in the front row where Elizabeth usually sat.

A short time later Elizabeth came in and sat right next to Harold. There were 850 empty seats, and she chose to sit next to Harold. Then Harold's girlfriend of the week came in and sat on the other side of him. Harold and his latest held hands and played kissy-face, while tears rolled down Elizabeth's cheeks. She continued to sit there and be even more deeply wounded instead of moving to one of the other 850 available seats.

I could hardly process what I was seeing as I continued to deliver my Sunday sermon. After service, as the social hour wound down, only a few people remained. Elizabeth, in a codependent puddle of emotion, was one of them. I did something I have never done before or since. I walked up to her, grabbed her by her shoulders, shook her lovingly but firmly, and yelled, "Wake up! Stop doing this to yourself! Stop it right now! Get up and move! Don't let yourself be abused a minute more! Get up and move!"

What Elizabeth needed to do immediately was to forgive herself again, again, and again.

When something happens, make a decision about how you are going to feel about it. Shout, cry, and scream. Do whatever it takes to purge your consciousness of the recorded message that says all you deserve is unacceptable behavior. It will take time and a lot of effort, but put one foot in front of the other until you walk into your new life.

Forgive yourself if you've ever allowed yourself to be abused. Forgive yourself if you were a nun for nineteen years and suppressed your own holiness to follow the rules.

From *A Path with Heart* by Jack Kornfield: "We human beings are constantly in combat, at war to escape the fact of being so limited, limited by so many circumstances we cannot control. But instead of escaping, we continue to create suffering, waging war with good, waging war with evil, waging war with what is too small, waging war with what is too big, waging war with what is too short or too long, or right or wrong, courageously carrying on the battle."

Genuine spiritual practice requires us to learn how to stop the war. This is the first step, but it must be practiced over and over until it becomes our way of being. When you start to get upset about anything say, "*No!* I'm going to stop that. I am not going to wage this internal war. I am stopping it." Do that until it becomes your way of being.

The inner stillness of a person who is truly at peace brings peace to all those he or she encounters, creating an interconnectedness in the web of life. To achieve this we must let go of all outside influences and look deeply within ourselves.

Mahatma Gandhi certainly understood this when he said, "I have only three enemies. My favorite enemy, the most easily influenced for the better, is the British Empire. My second enemy is the Indian people. They are far more difficult. But my most formidable enemy opponent is a man named Mohandas K. Gandhi. With him I seem to have very little influence."

To make ourselves more conscious and to stop the war we must purify our inner filters. Several years ago an older friend told me she'd heard from a "very reliable source" that Reverend Bob, a colleague of mine, had been observed stealing money out of the offering baskets after church. She may have expected me to roll my eyes and be shocked, but instead I said, "It isn't true. Whatever source it came from, it isn't true."

"How can you say that?" she blurted out.

"Because I know he is a spiritual man who wouldn't lift money from the offering. It would never happen." Reverend Bob may have had some foibles, as we all do, but he was not a thief. Of that I was certain.

Some years later my friend came to me one day and said she had been talking to the accuser's son, and he'd told her that his mother's dementia had gotten so bad that she was telling the most outrageous stories about everyone.

"So I asked him," she said to me, "do you think she used to tell stories on Reverend Bob?" And he replied that she told awful, made-up stories about Reverend Bob, including that he was stealing money out of the offering baskets.

I knew it wasn't true. When you have done your forgiveness work and have reached a peaceful state, you know people from the inside out. When we forgive regularly we begin to see the face of God in everyone, not the reflected face of our own ego.

Reverend Bob was a holy man, not a thief, and I intuitively knew that and was willing to assertively express my knowing. Our egos can jump on any scrap of gossip and then repeat it. Most often it isn't true, and even if it is, why would you waste your life on such nonsense? God has created you for a grander purpose. Rise up. Quit being small. Be holy. Get up and move!

A man is rich in proportion to the number of things which he can afford to let alone.

—HENRY DAVID THOREAU

FORGIVENESS IN ACTION: CONTEMPLATION

Spending time contemplating inspirational ideas lifts us emotionally and spiritually. When we take time to think a "high" idea and ruminate on every word, on how the idea can be applied in our life, then we grow and deepen. It is a way of creating spiritual understanding and depth.

Find a quiet, comfortable place where you won't be disturbed or interrupted. Take several deep breaths, and then read one of the statements that follow over and over, letting the meaning sink in deeper and deeper. Meditate at least fifteen minutes a day on these ideas:

God is love.
God loves me.
God's love fills my mind, heart, and soul.
God holds nothing against me.
God will never desert me.
God is always with me.

CHAPTER 9

Forgiveness and Dealing with Death

Forgiveness is the final form of love.

—REINHOLD NIEBUHR

One of the deepest and most meaningful Buddhist practices is called *powa*, a devotional time of forty-nine days during which one offers up a sacred practice for a loved one who has passed away. It offers the practitioner something tangible "to do" when the rawness of a new grief is unbearable.

The Buddhists believe the forty-nine days immediately following death are critically important to the departed one who is in an in-between state called the *bardo*. In the bardo realm, where we experience a life review, many illusions arise to lure the departed into difficult or meaningless engagements.

If a loved one on earth is praying for the deceased, then she is assisting him in moving away from the bardo's tempting illusions and into the light, into auspicious and beneficial experiences.

I have done this practice five times so far. It is done out of tremendous love and great devotion. It is a major commitment to devote seven weeks to a daily, focused prayer time for another. It is not done while shopping or driving the car or watching TV. One needs to set up a space in the home dedicated to this purpose.

Sit on a meditation cushion or a chair, have a flower or a lit candle nearby, and perhaps burn incense—whatever gives you a sense of peace and intention. Make certain the area is free from clutter. Sit quietly and in peace as you gently breathe and focus. Allow your breath to calm you as you open your mind, heart, soul—your entire being— to your beloved who has just passed.

Reach out to him, connecting your mind to his eternal mind, your heart to his eternal heart. Visualize great rays of light flowing from you to the essence of your beloved. Be as centered and as still as you possibly can. See if you can actually sense a connection. Hold that connection and continue to send light and love. Twenty minutes will do, forty-five to sixty minutes if you are a frequent meditator. According to the Buddhists, this practice brings loving blessings to the departed as well as an enormous sense of peace to the practitioner that he or she is being of actual value to the loved one.

I first practiced powa the day of my precious father's transition. At the time my grief was the greatest agony of my life. Nothing came close. My father was a very awake, quietly spiritual man with whom my soul was and is totally bonded. His departure made me feel as if my soul was ripped from my body. It was an upside-down time of utter loss and sorrow. But I knew of the powa practice, and I knew I had to do something, anything to assist him on his soul's journey and to center myself.

This highly ritualistic practice brought order and calm to my fractured world, and I pray it brought comfort to my precious father. This practice can also help bring comfort to the practitioner, who may feel deserted by the late loved one and have to work on forgiveness. Although I felt no need to forgive my father, I understand how it may be necessary for those who lose people close to them.

Next I practiced powa for a recently deceased member of my congregation. I was quite connected to both him and his wife. She and I did the practice for the forty-nine days, each in our own home. From the beginning it felt as if he weren't actually in the bardo, because neither his wife nor I could sense his essence. It seemed to me that he was instantaneously gone, but his wife and I both knew the prayers were going somewhere.

Doing this practice brought a great deal of comfort to the wife, who also worked on forgiveness for being "deserted" by him. A side benefit of regular meditation for any reason is that the need for forgiveness gradually diminishes, because the meditator is connecting with the infinite and realizes the earthbound pettiness of grudges and hurt feelings is meaningless.

Two sisters were extremely close. Having been raised in an unloving household, they turned to each other for care and support. Denise, the younger one, had been plagued since childhood with an increasingly debilitating condition that, when she was fifty years old, forced her to resign from her executive position in social services. It took two hours each morning to care for and bandage her severely swollen legs.

The pain from her autoimmune disease continually worsened, and the resulting depression allowed her little of the pleasures of life. The only exception was live theater, particularly ballet, which she adored. She had abandoned everything else, including her spiritual beliefs and practices. She was sick and wounded and lived with blinding pain.

One afternoon she, her partner, and a friend attended the matinee presentation of the ballet *Swan Lake*. While at the performance she suddenly collapsed and died in her partner's arms.

Her sister, Patricia; her lover; and all her friends, including me, were stunned. We all knew she'd been deeply unhappy. She felt her body had betrayed her; she'd spoken of wanting to die in order to get a fresh start in a new and healthy body. In the normal sense she did not take her own life, but those who knew her and loved her agreed she literally had willed herself to die.

I strongly believe in the power of our thoughts, and those of us close to Denise witnessed exactly what focused, determined thought can produce. Her death devastated her older sister. Sobbing, Patricia came to me and said over and over, "What can I do? What can I do?"

When she calmed down enough to listen, I explained to her first the power of forgiving her sister for leaving her and then I outlined the powa practice. The two of us already had a bond of mourning, having mourned together for another person in the past. Patricia said she would begin the practice that day, because her grief was so all encompassing, so I joined her for the following forty-nine days.

We both sensed Denise's essence as we engaged in the daily meditation. After about four weeks both of us stopped connecting with her. We discussed it and we knew she had moved on into the light, though we both continued the practice for the full time. Doing so isn't about following the rules; it's just about staying in the prayer practice to total completion.

When grief is all consuming and we feel there is nothing we can do about it, we must begin to forgive immediately and also begin the powa practice immediately. This practice is ancient and holy and brings blessings to our loved one and relief and solace to our weeping souls.

We can forgive those who have passed away, either for leaving or for past pain they have imparted, but forgiveness is perhaps most important for the living. Vincent, a pianist at my church, once said, "Be quick to forgive, slow to judge."

It is usually the opposite. We are quick to judge and slow to forgive, which leads to pain, suffering, and separation. Remember the old commercial where the actor hits himself on the forehead when recognizing his error and exclaims, "I could have had a V8."

Occasionally we are hit on the head with a cosmic two-by-four and inside us the words reverberate: "I could have forgiven." This situation could have had a different outcome if you had been quick to forgive and slow to judge. We are always choosing quick or slow.

The Zen Buddhists would turn this into a spiritual practice:

Quick or slow.
On the in-breath—quick.
On the out-breath—slow.

Do this seven times. It is a very helpful little practice. When we are slow in our anger or judgment and quick in our willingness to forgive, we are led to a peaceful life, a happy life. Therefore, we are always choosing whether we judge and hate or forgive and love. We choose to let go of whatever occurs, or to grab and hold on tightly.

To paraphrase a psychiatrist friend of mine, I have not been doing this for thirty-seven years, and listening to those sitting on my couch, without learning a thing or two. One of the things I've learned about people, even those who consider themselves to be spiritual, is that they can be quick to judge. I know I have to be very mindful of that tendency in myself.

We must constantly remind ourselves not to judge and to be quick to forgive. In the Dhammapada the Buddha tells us that he merely points the way. All the effort must be done by us.

We must be anchored in the truth because there will always be disasters and other terrible happenings in the world. My friends William and Marie in San Diego awakened to the news of the high school shootings in William's hometown of Chardon, Ohio. They found it almost incomprehensible.

I phoned them early that morning. William said the TV came on at seven a.m. to wake them as it does every morning. The sound was off. There was just the flickering of the light from the screen, which always awakened them. He was trying to read the scroll at the bottom of the screen without his glasses. To his astonishment he made out the word "Chardon." Fumbling for his glasses, he woke Marie, as together they watched in disbelief as the tranquility of his idealized hometown was shattered to bits.

We are always being made aware of the tragedies of life. In the United States alone there was 9/11, the Oklahoma City bombing, mass shootings in Colorado, the killing of innocent women in Cleveland, and—in my opinion the most horrendous of all—the murders of little children and their teachers at Sandy Hook Elementary School, in Newtown, Connecticut.

Jesus said, "The world you will have with you always." And unimaginably terrible horrors happen in the world.

To have any peace of mind we must be anchored in a higher reality. Without this touchstone we are going to be constantly devastated and lost, feeling hopeless and alone when tragedy strikes.

My spiritual teaching and understanding have always grounded me in this spiritual truth: There is no evil. You may or may not agree with this, but I know it in my soul. To say a disaster has to do with evil is naïve. The perpetrators are not evil; they are guided by what *A Course in*

Miracles calls "insane thoughts." They may be lost and very sick souls, but there is no devil making them act insanely. They are simply insane.

When such a tragedy strikes, people and the press ask, "What was the motive?" Like insane behavior could have a motive, a motive that could explain away the horror. The perpetrators are individuals whose egos have run amok, who have incredibly misguided (insane) reasons for the carnage they cause. There is no motive.

There is no bugaboo out there or within a person. There is no devil. There is free will, and there is insanity. There are lives dominated by the ego—individual egos and collective egos. There are masses of people asleep to the God that dwells within them, and they need to wake up and forgive.

The mother of one of the many children murdered at Sandy Hook said, "You have to forgive or you'll keep that hatred in your heart."

Forgive, forgive, forgive and you'll find peace and limitless love within your heart.

Jacqueline Herouard was in her native France on D-day, but her story, both tragic and romantic, did not begin then for the sixteen-year-old. It began several years earlier when she was ten and Germany invaded France.

The second youngest of eight children, she was living a carefree life in Le Havre. In her naïveté and innocence she had no way to grasp the idea of a Nazi force coming to their town and completely changing the course of life for her and her family.

But the Nazis did come to Le Havre and to their family store, which Jacqueline's mother and older siblings had been running since her father's death. The Nazis, whom Jacqueline always refers to as "the Germans," came, and they came with a ferocity.

When I questioned this gentle lady who had endured so much in her youth why she didn't refer to the invaders as "Nazis," she responded, "I don't know, maybe it was because they were a presence in France for so long. We just always called them 'the Germans.'"

Her whole family, including her married sisters and their husbands and one baby, lived above the family store. But then came the terrible day when several stern Germans were at the door, pounding loudly and barking orders in fractured French. Get out! You have one hour to get out!

They had no choice but to leave. Jacqueline carried one small valise with her meager belongings in it. The family walked away and spent the first night in a field where they heard bombs exploding all around them. Jacqueline found a rusty, discarded gas can, put it over her head, and held it tightly for protection all night long.

"I could never adequately explain what we went

through. France was not France anymore," she said through tears seventy-five years later.

With the family that first night were friends from Cherbourg. Five of them died in the bombings, so the survivors decided to leave the next evening for Saint-Lô, some one hundred miles away. With her little suitcase in hand she and her family walked and walked. "It took many days," she recalled.

Once at Saint-Lô the parish priest there sent them to an empty house where they were supposed to be safe. But the house was bombed that night. Death was everywhere, but miraculously the family was still intact. They left again, this time coming upon an empty barn.

They settled in for the night, and all seemed quiet until they heard the rats coming out. Jacqueline and her siblings were terrified of the scampering overhead. The little girl wanted to run from the barn, but her brother stopped her, telling her there was nowhere to go.

The family moved again into an old school that another local priest showed them. With other families they hid there for quite a long time, during which one sister and brother-in-law disappeared. Other family members searched for them for two weeks. Nothing. No word. No sightings. Finally the mother found them in a small rural clinic. They had been shot, but fortunately both of them survived.

The war raged around the family every day. Even from their hiding places they would see large, open trucks filled with Jewish people passing by. The family knew Jews were being rounded up, but they did not know why or to where they were being taken. With deep sadness Jacqueline said, "We had no idea. When I asked a fellow Le Havre resident in hiding if she knew what had become of my favorite music teacher, Mrs. Klein, she told me sadly she saw her leaving in a truck."

For the next several years they remained on the run and in survival mode. Two of Jacqueline's brothers had been arrested and were interned in POW camps for a total of five years. The rest of the family members, however, were finally able to return to their home above the general store and to reopen their retail establishment.

The Nazi occupation was in full force, so they were compelled to wait on heel-clicking, *Heil Hitler*–calling soldiers who simply took what they wanted, including the family's food coupons and Jacqueline's precious mandolin. But the family persevered and survived.

She choked up when with great feeling she said, "We knew the Americans were coming. We just knew it. We didn't know anything about when or how, but we all knew they were coming. That knowing kept hope alive in us."

One day Jacqueline and her sister were outdoors when her sister cried out, "Look up! Look up!"

"When I looked up," Jacqueline recalled, "all I could see everywhere were white parachutes floating to earth. I was overcome with emotion. The Americans were finally arriving."

It was June 6, 1944—D-day. She knew now there was a chance they would be liberated. There was a chance they would be free again. There was a chance France could be France once again. There was a chance her family could be reunited.

For the first time in years Jacqueline, by then in her teens, began to feel safe. After the Allied invasion, American and Canadian soldiers started coming into their store. She recalled with a laugh, "All they wanted was *parfum*, asking for Chanel No. 5. I'm convinced none of them knew anything about Chanel No. 5, just that they had been told to ask for it for the girl back home."

A few months later Jacqueline and her sister were about to fasten the upstairs shutters to their bedroom window for the night when they saw two American GIs looking up at them. "*Bonsoir, mademoiselles. Bonsoir, mademoiselles*," one of them said, butchering the pronunciation.

Giggling, they replied in unison, "*Bonsoir, monsieurs*."

The American, Nick Crea (my cousin's uncle), said to his buddy, "See that girl on the right? I'm going to marry her."

"Sure," his friend said sarcastically.

Confidently Nick retorted, "You just wait and see."

The next day Nick entered the store and asked for—of all things—Chanel No. 5. He spoke to sixteen-year-old Jacqueline in Italian, in which he was fluent and which she understood. He kept returning to the store, and Jacqueline's family teased her. They said they didn't think he was coming back for *parfum*.

After a number of visits to Jacqueline at the store, Nick asked her for a date. Her mother agreed, but only with a chaperone. They dated for thirteen months, and Nick then asked for her hand in marriage.

The parish priest at Sacré-Coeur church in Le Havre wrote (in Latin, no less) to his counterpart in Nick's hometown of Cleveland, Ohio. In the letter he asked what sort of person the suitor was. The response (also in Latin) from the Cleveland priest assured him that Nicholas was from an upstanding family, and that everyone in the family and the community was very proud of him and his involvement in the liberation of France.

Jacqueline and Nick were married by the Sacré-Coeur priest, then traveled to a Paris in ruins—but still Paris—for their honeymoon.

When Nick and his bride returned to the United States, Jacqueline recalls Americans telling her how hard they had it during the war with rationing and blackouts. She would simply nod in response, knowing they had no concept of the horrors she had survived. She would recall that first night with a gas can over her head and seeing a five-year-old Polish girl shot in the back simply because she was Polish.

"I've learned to forgive," Jacqueline said. "I'm good at forgiving. I don't dwell on or hate what the Germans did. I can talk about it now. Still there are images in my mind's eye that I try not to bring back. I can't erase them, but I can choose not to replay them."

Through daily prayer work, religious devotion, and a keen desire to be free of the horrible images that had haunted her youth, she forgave the Germans, just as the Dalai Lama had to learn to forgive the Chinese for what they had done to his people.

Few of us have had to forgive on a national or international scale. Few of us have had to endure the suppression of our life and liberty in the face of a dictator, be it Hitler or Mao.

If these two people can move to the place in consciousness where they can see their history as fodder for their souls' growth, cannot we be quick to do the same under far less life-threatening circumstances? No matter how offensive you have seen your perpetrator be, surely he was no Hitler or Mao.

The Buddha taught that suffering increases one's inner strength. Reflect on that wisdom in your own life and know that forgiveness will set you free as it has Jacqueline and the Dalai Lama.

Jacqueline concluded her story by saying, "My life with Nick was good. He was the love of my life, and he loved me from first sight. We were happily married for over fifty years before he passed. My story has a happy ending, because I am happy now." Forgiveness played a big part in setting her free to enjoy life and create that happy ending.

An interesting side note to her life: Jacqueline Herouard Crea has never seen a World War II movie. She doesn't need to; she lived it.

FORGIVENESS IN ACTION:
FINDING YOUR SAFE SELF

In a quiet moment go back into your history to a time you felt alone and frightened, perhaps when you were a young child.

Hold the memory of that child in your lap. Stroke that little one's head, caress the younger version of you, reassuring her or him, "You are safe now. Nothing is going to hurt you. I am in you. I am protecting you. You are safe. You are free." Feel the memory of your former self melt into your loving embrace. All is well.

CHAPTER 10

Your Personal North Star

*The key to successful spiritual practice is
never to lose your determination.*

—THE BUDDHA

In the Islamic tradition there is a belief that angels hover wherever green grows. It is an interesting belief for a people who came from predominately desert tribes.

We've already discussed that perhaps the most challenging aspect of forgiveness work is the forgiveness of self. When we do so, let us find the green and invite in our supportive helpers, our angels, to assist us.

Often we throw stones at ourselves and engage in self-destructive behavior. We overindulge in mind-altering substances. We run ourselves down in a pattern of negative self-talk. We work beyond our mental and physical limits to prove that we are worthy, lovable, capable.

We are worthy, lovable, capable—not because of what

we do but because of who we are. It is our God-given right. Everyone on Planet Earth has it equally, whether they believe so or not.

To achieve this knowing yourself, you must forgive anything and everything from your past that you feel makes you unworthy and keeps haunting your life. There is a place in you, the innermost part of you, where, regardless of anything and everything you have done in your past, you still remain as God created you.

This means that no matter what your past has been, no matter what you have made of the circumstances of your life, at your core you are holy and all other nonsense was just you in your asleep state pretending you were not holy. *A Course in Miracles* states, "Frightened people can be vicious." I have long interpreted this to mean that we can be vicious toward and against ourselves, as well as toward others.

How does viciousness toward oneself manifest? In my life, for instance, it showed up in a huge way as cancer. The basis, as I see it, was a highly dysfunctional relationship plus other dysfunctional relationships with varying degrees of intensity that, for a long time, I did my utmost not to look at.

Recently a spiritual soul sister of mine called asking for prayer support. She had just had a malignant growth removed from her face. The incised area was quite sore and sensitive, and the physician had removed a very wide margin "just to be safe." As we talked and prayed she said, "Actually I am not the least bit surprised. I have never liked my body and have always criticized many of my body parts. All that self-judgment had to come out somewhere."

I was more than a little shocked at what she said, because of all my attractive women friends she had always been the one who took the most care of herself. She was the most fit, stylishly groomed, and seemed to always be on top of self-care. It was curious to me that she did not see herself in that light at all.

She was conscious enough to immediately begin to forgive herself and alter her past self-judgments. She then started practicing loving every part of her body, all those parts she had previously viewed as flawed.

Our viciousness toward self can appear as illnesses, accidents, and poor choices in jobs, friendships, and romantic involvements. We put our time, talents, money, and most of all our consciousness in people and places where there are no satisfying outcomes.

To free ourselves and to get beyond these self-loathing cycles we must practice never-ending forgiveness. Also, take Jesus's message to "go and sin no more." Just quit doing it to yourself. Stop it!

Apologize to yourself as you might to a significant other. I'm sorry. Please forgive me. I love you. I'm sorry I've run you ragged. I'm sorry I've abused you. I'm sorry I settled for less than I deserve. I'm sorry I kept running and never paused long enough to really look at my life and my self-destructive behavior. I'm sorry I did not sufficiently honor you. I'm sorry I've been so sad.

We Are Not Here to Play Small

Years ago, when I was an unseasoned minister, a man with a sharp intellect in my congregation delighted in quizzing me each week. It became very tedious. For example, he would ask, "Sometimes you talk about going deeper. Sometimes you talk about going higher. Which is it?"

I would simply shake my head. "Obviously you have missed the teaching. It's both." I love the Buddha's teaching in which he talks about not going in two or four directions—like up or down, or east, west, north, or south—but ten. As we grow, we go further into the consciousness of forgiveness, moving in many directions.

Forgiveness is the function set for each one of us. Remember that your holiness has never left you, therefore you are the light of the world. It is your forgiveness that brings the world of darkness into the light. Forgiveness demonstrates you know the deepest truth about yourself—that you are the light of the world. Through forgiveness does the truth about yourself return to your memory.

Forgiveness is your liberator. The more you care for the happiness and well-being of others, the more your own sense of well-being will increase.

As we faithfully practice forgiveness we take on our true nature as daughters and sons of God. Then we join Jesus and the Buddha and Krishna and Muhammad and all the holy ones in being the light of the world.

Hopefully you are not the person you were five, ten, twenty, or fifty years ago. You may have made really unskilled decisions in the past. Why? The answer is simply because you didn't know how to do it differently. The truth is, when you know better you do better. You deserve a break. You deserve to cut yourself some slack, to give yourself a pass.

When we forgive ourselves fully we don't engage in that old behavior again. We change our way of thinking, speaking, being. We stop thinking negatively, speaking negatively, being negative.

In his book *Living Buddha, Living Christ*, Thich Nhat Hanh states the first precept of Buddhism:

Aware of the suffering caused by the destruction of life, I vow to cultivate compassion and learn ways to protect the lives of people, animals, plants, and minerals. I am determined not to kill, not to let others kill, and not to condone any act of killing in the world, in my thinking, and in my way of life.

Thich Nhat Hanh says that if we want to go north we use the North Star to guide us. If we want a happy, liberated life, we use forgiveness to guide us. How do we develop harmony in our lives? We become nonviolent in every sense of the word.

When we overwork ourselves and are frazzled, we must learn to stop. Then we must stop the judgments of ourselves and, as Paul McCartney sang, "Let it be." Or, as millions of young people sing today, "Let it go," from the song by Kristen Anderson-Lopez and featured in the movie *Frozen*.

Let us no longer let another human being take our joy away. Let us no longer give our joy away. Let us remember that it is our grievances that hide the light in us. Let us resolve to hide the light no more.

Let each of us take our rightful place in the transformation of the planet by letting our inner light shine. What an incredible place our world will be when we all learn to do that.

I know a gentle, soft-spoken woman who was once again hurting herself by being in a dysfunctional relationship. Her partner was particularly verbally abusive. He was always raging and carrying on, and she would cower while he ranted. When he started she would run around and close all the windows in the apartment so the neighbors would not hear his shouts.

One day he yelled at her, "You are a fucking idiot!"

She stopped in her tracks and looked at him. Then slowly within her the light dawned. And she smiled and she shouted back at him, "You're right! I am a fucking idiot!" Then she ran around the house opening all the windows. As she opened each one she shouted out, "I am a fucking idiot! I am a fucking idiot!"

And then she left.

And then she forgave herself.

And then she forgave him.

And then she was happy and peaceful and ready for a joyful life.

Albert Einstein was attributed as saying: "There are only two ways to live life. One is as though nothing is a miracle. The other is as though everything is a miracle."

We decide daily, perhaps moment by moment, which it is. We decide how we are going to think, how we are going to act, how we are going to live.

Luke 17:4: "'If he sins against you seven times in a day and seven times comes back to you and says "I repent," forgive him.'"

Matthew 18:21–22: "Then Peter came to Jesus and asked, 'Lord, how many times shall I forgive my brother when he sins against me? Up to seven times?' Jesus answered, 'I tell you not seven times, but seven times seventy times.'"

This command would have seemed outlandish to Jesus's followers. But the endless repetition of forgiveness acts opens our minds and clears our hearts for a new and glorious energy to present itself.

As I have taught, seven times seventy does not equal 490 times, but, rather, it equals the perfect number of times that it takes to clear the slates of our minds. It is work and not for the faint of heart or weak of will. It is work because it takes a whole lot of effort to shift our consciousness. Remember those ten thousand hours.

Years ago I was taught a forgiveness technique by a Unity minister from New Zealand, which I've detailed in the exercise at the end of this chapter. It uses forgiveness techniques for seventy times seven—meaning seventy times a day for seven days. Repeating acts of forgiveness cleans and opens our minds, making them receptive vehicles for future and desired good. When we are willing to do the true work of forgiveness, our lives take on a deep calm, and we are no longer disturbed by external events. What happened in the past no longer matters. It (whatever it is) no longer matters when you are free. It does matter when you are bound.

Forgiving and Moving On

Connie and I first met when she walked into my church over thirty years ago with her two towheaded toddlers. Her oldest child, a young son, was not with her. She was a registered nurse, soft-spoken and sincere, with a quiet intensity about her. And she was starving for spiritual nourishment.

She was married to an active alcoholic. She and her husband appeared to be polar opposites—she the responsible one and he the carefree, jolly drunk.

When Connie graduated from college, she moved to Sierra Leone to teach French. She and her future husband had dated briefly after high school and had stayed more or less in touch. She never forgot the bad boy as, in the meantime, he went to seminary school, only to be expelled from it. Even with all his foibles, she was drawn to his intelligence and moral fiber.

They were both raised in strongly religious families. Her father was a Methodist minister and his a deacon in the Catholic Church. David never pushed her to be sexually intimate with him. For both of them their families and church life were very important. She said that their early relationship was built on "passionate friendship."

Just before she was to leave for Africa the two of them went out and had sex in the back of his car. It was horrible for her. She bled so badly she thought she would have to go to the emergency room. Then a policeman knocked on the window and demanded, "What's going on?" Horrible. Even with that dismal bon voyage experience, after Connie left for Africa she could not get David out of her system.

Once in Sierra Leone, she fell in love—not with a man but with the country. Although foreign to this girl from Canton, Ohio, everything felt familiar. She felt as though she had been there before. She adored her years in Africa, had a new boyfriend, traveled, had life-altering experiences. Through it all, however, she could not get thoughts of David out of her consciousness.

By the time she returned to the United States he was living in Vienna, Austria. She contacted him and they picked up their relationship from a distance. After some time he proposed to her over the phone. She accepted, and it was decided that he would return to the States for the wedding, so her minister father could walk his only daughter down the aisle before stepping forward and officiating the ceremony.

After their wedding in Canton, she went with David to Vienna. It was in Vienna that it finally hit her how alcohol was more important to him than anything else. While there she told a friend that David sold Coke on the street. In shock her friend said, "Wow, you guys must be rolling in money."

Laughing aloud, Connie replied, "Not that kind of coke. He has a small pushcart with Coca-Cola and makes deliveries to all the local bars." According to Connie, it was his dream job. Each barkeep would give him a free drink or a beer, and he would arrive home drunk every night. Life was not good, and it wouldn't get better.

Then David got a job as a nightclub and tavern manager in Dublin, Ireland. Before they moved there they were on vacation in Spain, where Connie became pregnant. She was overjoyed, thrilled to be expecting. The nurse at the hospital who delivered the news to Connie, seeing her exuberance, said in a very detached manner, "Not the normal reaction I get from delivering such news to young women here."

Throughout the pregnancy David's drinking continued to escalate, and still Connie continued to think he was the most fascinating person she had ever met. Why? Intellectually he was brilliant, and he had a quick wit and charming manner that fit so well in Ireland.

When it was time to deliver, the Dublin hospital experience filled Connie with trepidation. Sixteen women were in a dimly lit public ward, all in different stages of labor or postdelivery, some hysterical, some panic-stricken. She described it as "a scene out of a really bad movie."

Nurse care was nonexistent. When her newborn son was brought to her for the first time, Connie said, "He's all wet."

"Yes," came the retort, "that's because you haven't changed his nappy." This was the first time she had seen her son, so how could she have changed his nappy?

In the meantime, where was the daddy? He was at the pub around the corner. When he finally staggered in, he announced that he sure hoped they were out of there by

Saturday, because he had a golf outing in another town and he was going no matter what!

As misery would have it, they were released on Saturday, and David was nowhere to be found. Connie had previously attended one meeting of the American Women's Club of Dublin, so she called them and sheepishly explained that she was in the hospital with a newborn son and her husband was out of town. She asked if anyone could possibly pick them up and give them a lift to the apartment. An American woman came to pick her and the baby up, but didn't speak a word to Connie, then dropped the two of them off at the curb. Connie was embarrassed and mortified.

In reflection many years later, Connie said that, of all David's dastardly deeds and behavior, going golfing and leaving her and their newborn son to beg for a ride home eclipsed everything else he had done before or would do in the future. The cake he had left in the apartment hardly made up for his absence. And yet, like so many women whose names are legion, she continued to stay, having two more children and ignoring the writing on the wall.

When I asked this now empowered, lovely woman why in the name of God she'd chosen to stay so long and have more children, she responded that she firmly believed (and still believes) she was supposed to have those additional babies and experiences. Connie knew what she did and she was doing the best she could at any moment.

As time passed, she had an insight that everyone was playing their parts. It was all a scene in the great script of her life and their lives. She could begin to look at it in a very analytical way, a very Buddhist way.

When Connie came to the Unity church, she learned how she could actually forgive her past to such a degree that it no longer had a choke hold around her neck and soul. She was what I call a "spiritual sponge." She became a voracious reader, studying metaphysical and spiritual teachings. She formed new, healthy relationships. She went to Al-Anon and met other people like herself, people who were getting on with their lives and were no longer defined by their alcoholic partner.

Connie was waking up and was at last finished with David. She said to him, "I finally feel done with you. I'm okay. I did everything I had to do. We are done."

In her healing process she had a mystical experience in which she literally felt the movement of grace. "I felt wrapped in the love of God. I now know the Holy Spirit as the comforter and what that means."

A longtime friend commented on how different she had become, no longer sarcastic or carrying buried anger. But, she said, "It seems like so much work!"

Connie replied, "It is so much work. It's daily work. It's never-ending."

Today, upon reflection, she recalls her years abroad and the experiences that formed what she calls "my strange little story." She now knows David not taking mother and baby home from the hospital was the defining moment of her life that, in order to move on, she had to forgive.

Connie is now exquisitely happy in her marriage to her second husband, Tim. Her friends and family believe that the reason she so adores him is that, after years with David, new husband Tim seems so "normal."

She recently retired from the major medical facility in Cleveland, Ohio, where she had been a charge nurse for over thirty years. In the blossoming of retirement she has undertaken doula training, being unable to stay out of a helping profession for long. She is such a happy person that one would never guess she had such a horrendous past.

As my early teacher Dr. Jean Houston would say, Connie is now a holy person and no longer a person filled with holes.

The Miracle of Forgiveness

A family I have been connected with my entire life experienced a miracle only forgiveness can bring. The three sisters had been estranged from their only brother for over fifteen years. During that time he had moved to Las

Vegas and he'd become clean and sober, yet he wanted nothing to do with his family.

Life went on without him for many years, and the two sisters I am closest to did a great deal of forgiveness work around the situation. I have noticed through the years that the most troublesome history to forgive is with family members, be they siblings or parents. Why? Perhaps, as well as sharing DNA, we share a history, a dining room table, a bathroom, relatives, a neighborhood, a school, family interests, family prejudices, and attitudes. We share karma.

My sister friends felt their forgiveness work was complete and rarely thought of their brother. But after years of no contact, he called one of them. Then he announced, "I need help. I have terminal cancer. I have no one. My nineteen-year-old girlfriend said she could not deal with my 'bag' any longer and left me [he's over fifty]. I need you back in my life. Can you forgive me and let me back in?"

Of course she said yes.

The three sisters conferred and agreed that what had happened in the past didn't matter. What mattered was that he was back and had a deep need. Each of the sisters had worked through the years on forgiveness and it had worked. Forgiveness had offered the sisters a new lease on life with their younger brother. So the time they had left together was experienced in meaningful ways and with love, rather than in pain, anguish, and separation.

It has been observed by spiritual practitioners that the principle of karma can have a great deal to do with how interconnected our relationships with family members are. We are not related to those siblings, parents, grandparents, aunts, uncles, and cousins by some random chance or cosmic roll of the dice.

When in our spiritual evolution we can view our relations from a higher perspective, our lives can then come into much clearer focus. The four siblings caught the higher vision and knew there was a whole lot more going on than their personalities would lead them to believe. There are reasons, known and unknown, as to why they chose this particular dance of life.

So what became of the four siblings? One of the sisters, a nurse, went to Las Vegas to stay with her brother through his four surgeries and his radiation and chemotherapy treatments. She had only compassion for him and embodied the teaching that what had happened in the past no longer mattered.

We all prayed and prayed. Miracles do happen. At that time Jon was told the cancer was in remission. He would have to wear a colostomy bag for the rest of his life, but all evidence of the disease appeared to be gone.

Did he have to change his lifestyle? Yes.

Did he have to change his attitudes? Yes.

Did he have to change his mind? Yes.

Did he have to drop a lot of his egotistical ways? Yes.

Did he become more peaceful and content than he had ever been? Yes.

Did he understand that it was quite extraordinary that he had lived through stage 4 cancer? Yes. His life wasn't the same, but it was different and much, much better. Sadly the remission didn't last forever and he passed away. But his sisters all thanked God that they had made amends. And I know he was grateful for the renewed connection with his sisters as he moved on to his next adventure.

Practice the seventy times seven exercise below whenever you are confronted with a pesky problem and see what miracles come into your life.

FORGIVENESS IN ACTION:
SEVENTY TIMES SEVEN

Years ago I was taught a forgiveness technique by a Unity minister from New Zealand:

> I, [your first name], now forgive myself for all
> known and unknown limitations I have placed
> on myself or others.

Close your eyes, breathe deeply, relax, contemplate the words, connect with them. Once you have done this and are in a deep state of relaxation, begin writing the above forgiveness statement. I suggest you write it longhand seventy times a day for one week.

You can be creative as to how you do it. I use a legal pad and carry it with me wherever I go: I write at a long red light, waiting five minutes for a friend at lunch, waiting for an appointment, or while on hold on the phone. Or you can simply turn off your cell phone, computer, TV, radio, and any other noisy distraction and write.

Do it thoughtfully, mindfully. This practice still remains one of the best means I know of to vacuum clean your soul of all unhealed memories. You don't have to minutely reexamine every miserable episode of your life. You can liken it to taking out the garbage once a week. Before you take it to the curb, you don't reopen each garbage bag to remind yourself what you are throwing away. It's knowing, yes, there are old issues in there oozing into my present life. I don't want or need them anymore.

CHAPTER 11

Making Amends

You can't forgive without loving. And I
don't mean sentimentality. I don't mean mush.
I mean having enough courage to stand up
and say, "I forgive. I'm finished with it."

—MAYA ANGELOU

Even if you feel you did nothing wrong, or that you were not the responsible party, doing several amends practices can be helpful to your overall, complete healing. Sometimes we allow ourselves to mentally engage in regretful situations.

If you have done a great deal of the forgiveness exercises taught in this book, and still the energy has not substantially shifted, here are a few additional ways to go even deeper on your journey to freedom.

Do a thoughtful, kind act for someone who has absolutely nothing to do with the issue. Maya Angelou said she would make an entire Sunday dinner for someone not involved in her situation, deliver it, and say, "I made this dinner for you in my attempt to forgive Jimmy completely." An act such as this will help shift the energy by putting a tangible blessing on another person.

A few other ideas might be:

- Bake a cake and give it away.
- Bake a batch of cookies and give them away.
- Buy movie tickets and snack vouchers for a family who normally couldn't afford to go to the movies.
- Offer to clean a friend's home, garage, or car.
- Mow your elderly neighbor's lawn.
- When going through a tollbooth, give the attendant $20 or $30 extra and ask that the money be used to pay as many tolls for other drivers as he or she can. (This works best for short toll roads, rather than long ones like the Pennsylvania Turnpike.)

You get the idea, and you can certainly come up with many creative ideas of your own. Remember to communicate, "I am doing this to fully forgive Jimmy."

Once when I was at a local Starbucks my cappuccino was paid for by a kind stranger. That simple act put a smile on my face and made me feel appreciative for the kindness of others.

Of course you can always do a kind act for the very person. I suggest you do it anonymously so your ego or your desire to be right does not get involved. Once, when an extremely close friend of mine closed me out of her life with no explanation or contact ever again, I sent her a most beautiful silk scarf for her birthday. It took a bit of maneuvering, but there was no clue the gift was from me.

Whatever kind gesture you choose to make, either to the person involved or to someone not involved, put no expectation or emotional strings on the gift. Do it, let it go, and allow the spirit to do the deeper work.

The most difficult acts of forgiveness are those for people we have been deeply involved with or attached to. It is not the casual acquaintance or the annoying coworker who has access to our soul and can wound it. Like Jesus, the Judases of our lives are nearly always those with whom we have been the closest, the ones who have gained entry into our hearts.

It is not the guy down the block, it is our brother, the aunt we trusted, who betrayed that trust. Those are our teachers. When we move to the place where we can see them as teacher rather than as enemy, then we have a chance at healing our wounds and our souls.

When you do an anonymous, kind gesture toward

that person or in the name of that person, enfold that act in prayer and light. Then you can begin to experience a shift inside you—if not the first time, then the fifth or the ninth. Always remember you are performing these magnanimous acts to shift your own consciousness, not the other person's.

On numerous occasions I have heard the Dalai Lama teach that our meditations, our spiritual practices, are about changing us and very seldom do they change the other person. The other person will change because he wants to, not because you want him to.

The Buddha said, "To conquer oneself is a greater task than conquering others."

But we must consistently do our spiritual practices. We get up early and meditate. We study sacred texts. We listen to and learn from enlightened teachers to liberate our souls from the burdens of the past.

If others are lifted up as a secondary result of our journey, that is wonderful and good. But it should not be our primary goal, because that will lead to disappointment and frustration.

Conquer your own mind. Sometimes when dealing with small matters, it's not too difficult. But many times it is an enormous task, and for most of us it requires an enormous amount of willingness and spiritual discipline.

Remember, we forgive because we need to forgive, not because the other is worthy or wants to be forgiven or is sorry (which is rarely the case). We forgive without ceasing because it is the spiritual thing to do. It is the only thing we can and must do. We must do it for as long as it takes and as frequently as the situation demands.

When Everything Goes Wrong

Generally speaking my life flows in an orderly fashion. "Divine order," I call it. It is usually quite clear that God is in charge, but when my husband and I finally made the decision to move to Hawaii, everything that could go wrong went wrong—and then some. It was dystopia to the max.

The first thing we did was put our home on the market. Then we arranged for a top estate-sale team to handle the disbursement of most of our possessions. The sale was set for the weekend before Thanksgiving. We moved out of our home and in with a minister friend who lived on the other side of Cleveland.

Then the weather turned wicked—blizzards with many inches of snow and subzero temperatures. It was the worst winter in the Cleveland area in 136 years.

The sale was a bust. We thought we would net many thousands of dollars. We lived in a gated neighborhood, so only a few people were permitted in at a time for the sale. To make things worse, neighbors called the police because they did not want "strangers" inside the gates. The estate-sale company said it was the worst sale and worst conditions they had ever encountered, even though they had done significant advertising. We netted a tiny fraction of what our possessions were worth.

We continued to drive the forty-five miles to and from our house three to four times a week in an attempt to sell as much of our stuff on our own as we could. We sold a few things, but all in all we were as unsuccessful as the estate-sale people were.

The weather continued to be horrendous. Many roads were nearly impassable, and some were closed. At one point, we couldn't get to our house for four days. When we finally did, and my husband and I entered through our garage, there was the ominous sign of ice on the garage floor. When David opened the kitchen door from the garage, the sound of gushing water filled his ears. He couldn't believe what his eyes saw. Water poured down from the second floor. Pipes had burst.

I entered through the front door and encountered a saunalike atmosphere. In the kitchen, part of the ceiling had collapsed, and two antique tables below had been smashed. The beautiful French wallpaper was hanging in sheets from the walls. The dining room was flooded; floorboards were soaked and warped. And on and on the damage went. David and I were stunned, numb, disbelieving at the sad scene.

I immediately called our insurance agent. His secretary told me the policy had been canceled for nonpayment! Apparently our forwarded mail had been inconsistent, and we had not received the bill at our temporary residence. I cried to the secretary, "Couldn't someone have called us? I've been with him for thirty-five years."

"Sorry," she said. Half of our house was destroyed, and due to a series of strange circumstances we had no insurance. Dystopia: Anything that could go wrong, did.

Shortly after that I was diagnosed with a life-threatening condition and went into the hospital. Fortunately it was caught in time, and I was given medication, which kept it at bay. It was obviously no surprise to me that this health challenge arose on the heels of everything else that was going on.

My doctor recommended that I retire immediately because of the fragile nature of my health. It was as though I was inside someone else, because this certainly didn't feel like my life. It was a nightmare. My church and its leadership felt that they were not prepared to go on without me. So the church closed, owing me a substantial sum of money. I was paid enough for a couple of weeks' worth of groceries. This was not my life.

Family and friends who knew about the situation exclaimed that they had never seen anything of such biblical proportions. Several used the Italian word *malocchio*, for evil eye, or a curse someone puts on a person they wish to harm. That isn't something I would put much credence in, but, my heavens, something was going on.

A very spiritual friend of mine did some core soul work on me and then instructed me to write the 91st Psalm each night in longhand. I told him that an element of my nighttime prayers is saying the 23rd Psalm. He told me to write out the 91st Psalm every night until I felt the energy shift. I was miserable and desperate, so I followed instructions and wrote and wrote and wrote. It's not a short psalm.

On the twenty-first night I felt the energy shift and my consciousness lighten. I continued to write for several nights more until I knew I was complete. As my energy shifted I once again was able to live in my dream and not in someone else's nightmare.

I offer this ancient Old Testament technique, which comes from the teachings of the Kabbalah. Some of the old teachings are very meaningful and powerful because they have been practiced for millennia.

So if you feel you've lost control of your life, every day or night write the 91st Psalm in longhand. Why the 91st? I don't know, but don't intellectualize it, just do it. All it takes from you is a willingness to do it.

When you write the 91st, make it your sole/soul focus—no TV, headphones, computer, or iPhone. It's just you, the Bible, pen, and paper. Pay attention to what you're doing. Do it prayerfully, mindfully. Do it daily for as long as necessary. It will take at least a week, probably longer. When your load begins to lighten, write for a few more days and give thanks that you have arrived at a gentler crossroads.

The Courage to Make Amends

Making amends takes courage, which is a prerequisite for most endeavors in life. It takes courage to live in this world. It takes courage to speak truth, and it takes even more courage to live according to the highest ideals of your heart. And courage can move the act of making amends to its highest level, as in the following story, which comes from Nigel Taylor, an Australian and a spiritual teacher friend of mine.

Weary Dunlop was an Australian doctor who lived through the Second World War. Much has been written about him, but something not often spoken about was this story as it was shared on the radio by a one-time friend of Weary's. He had served with him in Burma during the war. And he spoke of Weary Dunlop's great courage.

Weary, who had been captured by the Japanese, was a leader and medical doctor during the infamous building of the Burma–Thailand Railway. Many times his fellow prisoners of war would simply fall with sickness from heat, disease, or any number of other ailments. Weary would attend to them. His captors repeatedly cautioned him not to. He ignored them, to such an extent that the commanding officer of the camp forced Weary, a tall man who towered over his captors, to dig a hole in the hard rock, in the burning sun, so that he would stand eye to eye with the considerably shorter commander.

When Weary had dug the hole to a sufficient depth, the commander beat him harshly with a rattan. The other prisoners rose up and were ready to storm the guards and rescue Weary. But he raised his hand and directed them to stop. The beating continued.

After the Japanese surrendered, Weary, along with the rest of the survivors, was released and he returned to Australia. Postwar reconstruction began in 1946, and there was a call sent out for people to volunteer to go to Japan to help rebuild the country. Weary was the first to step forward. He led a team of doctors into Japan to help heal the wounds, at all levels of being, of the everyday man, woman, and child who lived in the remains of that war-torn country.

His friend shared Weary's reasoning on the radio. He quoted Weary as saying, "How can we ever hope to rebuild a world of peace if I cannot even forgive my captors?" And off he went, spending the rest of his life dedicated to helping those in need, right up to his passing in 1993.

Dr. Weary Dunlop embodied the fullness of the purest teachings on forgiveness, as he lived his inner convictions to the fullest. Weary was a man who completely manifested compassion, forgiveness, and how to be of service to the very end. May we all aspire to such unconditional love as he demonstrated.

FORGIVENESS IN ACTION:
MAKING AMENDS

In this chapter I've outlined several ways to make amends, whether directly or indirectly. Choose one, and begin to do it today. Take time in your journal to expand on how that practice you've chosen unfolds in your life.

I highly suggest you do the seventy times seven technique as well as actually writing the 91st Psalm for a number of times until the light dawns upon the situation.

CHAPTER 12

Beyond Forgiveness

Forgive, you will have happiness. Forgive, you will have
satisfaction. Forgive and forget, you will have
everlasting peace within and without.

—SRI CHINMOY

Of all the remarkable forgiveness stories I've heard, the tale of Tibetan monk Lopon-la is without equal.

After the Dalai Lama was able to escape from Tibet, Lopon-la was imprisoned in the capital, Lhasa, where he remained behind bars for an unbelievable eighteen years. His crime was being a Buddhist monk. Over the years he was frequently tortured and forced to renounce his religion.

When at last he was released, he traveled to Dharamsala, India, to see the Dalai Lama. His Holiness had not seen the monk for twenty years but, he reflected (as quoted by Victor Chan in the book *The Wisdom of For-*

giveness), "He seemed the same. Of course looked older. But physically OK. His mind still sharp after so many years in prison. He was still same gentle monk. . . . I asked him whether he was ever afraid. Lopon-la then told me: 'Yes, there was one thing I was afraid of. I was afraid I may lose compassion for the Chinese.' I was very moved by this, and also very inspired."

The Dalai Lama said that, because of his unwavering faith and his focus on forgiveness while in prison, Lopon-la's experience with his captors did not change him for the worse. He was able to survive those torturous years without his soul and mind being damaged. Absolutely re-markable and inspiring.

On a recent Memorial Day David and I invited several people over for brunch. I had the idea of each of us shar-ing meaningful memories centered around this holiday. When it was my turn I told the story of my uncle Phil Gibbons.

Phil was an Army Air Force pilot during World War II, and his plane was shot down over the Netherlands. He bailed out, but shortly after he landed he was captured by the Nazis. He spent the next two and a half years in a POW camp before being freed after the Allied invasion.

How I wished I had more of the details of his story, but he did not want to talk about his harrowing experi-ences. However, my aunt Delores told me he went through a living hell at the hands of the Nazis.

Initially his family thought he was dead, but a seren-dipitous happening changed that. His brother had gone to a movie in Boston, and in those days before television, newsreels were shown ahead of the movie. On this partic-ular occasion the newsreel showed captured Nazi footage of SS guards with prisoners. One of the prisoners was my uncle Phil. I have a still photo taken from the film, which shows this tall, lean young man flanked by SS guards who barely come up to his shoulder. One can see his right fist tightly clenched in the photo.

Did he practice forgiveness for his experiences at the hands of the Nazis? I'll never know for sure, but I suspect he did some work to free his psyche. He was neither a mean nor an embittered man, and he always did what he believed to be right and just.

After he retired as a colonel from the air force, he created a series of tours to take retired GIs back to Eu-rope so they could revisit many of the places where they had fought during the war. He led these tours for more than a dozen years.

For many who traveled with Phil to Europe it was a healing experience, as it had to be for Phil. Revisiting sites in peacetime where war once raged changes one's per-spective. In 1944 the beaches of Normandy were littered with blood and bodies, and fear and hatred abounded. Today those same beaches are wide and beautiful, and peace is everywhere.

So did my uncle Phil forgive? I don't know if he called it that, but of course he did and he happily moved on with the rest of his life.

W Mitchell (whom I mentioned in the introduction) was also a guest at this brunch. Getting him and his wheelchair up the garage steps and into our home was a bit of a challenge for my husband and another male guest, who were in front and at the rear of Mitchell's chair, pushing and pulling. One of them almost missed a step and lurched, jostling Mitchell in the chair. "Easy, guys," Mitchell said calmly in a droll voice, "I'm not known to have the best of luck." We all laughed heartily, Mitchell made it into the house, and we all enjoyed the afternoon and early evening.

As a very cocksure young man, Mitchell had purchased the largest, most expensive, meanest motorcycle available. The next morning he fulfilled a lifelong dream by soloing in an airplane for the first time. That afternoon, astride his brand-new adored bike, he was tooling down a street in San Francisco when a laundry truck turned left in front of him and he plowed into it. He crushed his elbow and cracked his pelvis as he hit the pavement. But the worst of it was the lid on the gas cap popped open and two and a half gallons of gasoline poured onto him and the hot engine and was ignited.

He was in the middle of a pillar of fire four feet wide and ten feet high. He was burned over 65 percent of his body, and despite all odds, with endless skin grafts, facial reconstruction, four months in the hospital, and two years in rehabilitation, he lived.

A few weeks after reading his book, we spotted Mitchell again coming out of the laundry room. We introduced ourselves and told him how moved and inspired we were by his story. I said I'd like to ask him a question. He immediately responded, "Whatever the question is, the answer is 'Yes.'" That was a first for me. I then told him I was writing a book on forgiveness and would be honored to interview him. Of course he agreed, because I already knew his answer was "Yes."

A few days later we met on his lanai. Mitchell was the most physically damaged human being I had ever seen. There was ample evidence of all the skin grafts and reconstructive surgery he had endured. He never wore a shirt. (Although I suspected it was because of the pain clothing might have caused, I didn't want to be so personally invasive as to ask why.) His chest, neck, and face looked like a patchwork quilt. And he had no fingers on either hand. No fingers!

After his motorcycle accident, Mitchell was able to walk again and return to a fairly normal life. Then the unthinkable happened. Mitchell was once again piloting a plane, this time with several passengers aboard, and the plane lost power and crash-landed on the runway. Everyone aboard was slightly injured, except for Mitchell, whose spine was crushed, leaving him paraplegic for the remainder of this incarnation.

While still in ministerial school I learned that, whenever I felt uneasy faced with the evidence of another person's physical suffering like this, it was best just to look into their eyes. I did that and began to ask Mitchell to share his experiences of forgiveness. He responded that he really hadn't worked on forgiveness a lot. Surprised, I replied, "With everything you have had to endure, you have nothing to forgive?"

"No," he said calmly. "I never judged either event as bad or wrong or what it should not be. Before the two accidents I took a course called 'Morehouse.' It was quite popular years ago in California. There I learned that everything that happens is how it had to be. It is just perfect in all its seeming flaws and injustices. It is all how it had to be for some higher order to manifest. I could see my life as a catastrophe or a challenge. I chose the latter."

"Wow," I responded, "that is not in any way dissimilar to what we teach and live in Unity. But the extent to which you are manifesting this eternal truth is beyond anything I have ever witnessed. Mitchell, you are not one in a million. You are one in a billion."

He loved what I said. A Tibetan rinpoche had told Mitchell he was an enlightened man. He loved that, too. The rinpoche added that Mitchell had agreed to come to this incarnation as a teacher.

W Mitchell glows with the light of God. He is witty, laughs easily, and is openhearted and quite awake. In all my decades of ministry and ministering, I have never met anyone who seems so beyond the need to practice forgiveness, or anyone so successfully free of judgment, living life fully with no regrets.

The legions whom I have counseled, supported, and taught have not had to endure one one-hundredth of what Mitchell has. And yet they feel, all too often, put upon, victimized, unloved, betrayed. With his attitude, faith, and inner fortitude, he is inspiring thousands. He certainly inspired me. He shows us that we are not our bodies. He demonstrates that what is within us is greater than anything or any occurrence in the world. May we all emulate W Mitchell.

But until we do, may we all practice forgiveness—endlessly.

The Power of Forgiveness is filled with numerous forgiveness practices and techniques that have brought freedom from separation, and liberation from suffering, to countless people.

FORGIVENESS IN ACTION:
GRATEFULNESS

As we conclude, take time for one more list. Ponder what you have in your life for which to be grateful.

Write it down; think and write; contemplate and write; remember and write.

Walk away from the list for a few days, then reread it and add to it.

Meditate, hold the list in your lap, and be happy.

Many ideas that work have been presented here for you. But remember, as the Buddha said, "All the work has to be done by you." No matter to what degree you must do the work to be free, it is well worth it.

If you want to live a happier life, a freer life, a healthier life, a more spiritual life, be willing to do the work and set yourself free. You are worth all the effort. You do deserve it.

May every blessing be upon you and all that you do.

Acknowledgments

First and foremost, from the depths of my heart, I acknowledge my soul mate and husband, David Alexander. You are brilliant at reading my scrawl and turning it into sentences, paragraphs, and pages—all with correct punctuation. In so many ways my books are our books.

Next I acknowledge Anne Sibbald, who has been my literary agent for more than twenty years and gets my message. You are a friend.

Publisher Joel Fotinos of Tarcher, who has always honored my teaching and encouraged me to do even more, has also become a dear friend.

Joel's assistant, Brittany Gilbert, has respectfully and skillfully crafted this book through all its stages. You are always so tactful and easy to work with.

I want to thank my dear friends and former congregants who have loved me for so many years—especially Sandy Deck, Rudi Barnes, and Felicia Martinez.

I acknowledge all of my students for the important role you have played in my life. I would not be the spiritual teacher I am without you. Thank you.

Bestselling author Joan Gattuso brings deep spiritual insight into all of her writing. She began learning the deepest lessons of forgiveness through early soul lessons of betrayal and injustice. She learned what it truly means "to turn the other cheek" and forgive one's adversaries. She has come to understand and teach that everything—without exception—can and must be forgiven. In *The Power of Forgiveness* she skillfully and gently guides the reader to do so in his or her own life. Joan has studied with the great teachers of the twentieth and twenty-first centuries on her spiritual path, which has taken her around the world, and she incorporates their wisdom into her body of work, which includes *A Course in Love*, *A Course in Life*, and *The Lotus Still Blooms*. She lives in Hawaii with her husband, David Alexander.